Ripley's
Believe It or Not!®
WEIRD-ITIES!

Publisher Anne Marshall
Editorial Director Rebecca Miles
Assistant Editor Charlotte Howell
Text Geoff Tibballs
Proofreader Judy Barratt
Picture Researchers James Proud, Charlotte Howell
Art Director Sam South
Senior Designer Michelle Foster
Reprographics Juice Creative

Executive Vice President Norm Deska
Vice President, Archives and Exhibits Edward Meyer

Published by Ripley Publishing 2013
Ripley Publishing, Suite 188, 7576 Kingspointe Parkway,
Orlando, Florida 32819, USA

2 4 6 8 10 9 7 5 3 1

ISBN 978-1-60991-026-6

Some of this material first appeared in *Ripley's Believe It or Not! Expect... The Unexpected*

Library of Congress Cataloging-in-Publication data is available

Manufactured in China in February/2013 by Leo Paper
1st printing

Ripley's Believe It or Not!

WEIRD-ITIES!

WEIRD AND WONDERFUL

Ripley
PUBLISHING
a Jim Pattison Company

PAGE
12

PAGE
15

WEIRD AND WONDERFUL

Against the odds. The most amazing art,
outrageous festivals, and bizarre bodies
are packed into this extraordinary book.
Meet the father and son with six toes
on each foot, the artist who paints by
hearing colors, and the brave contestants
at the Bug Eating Championships.

PAGE
26

PAGE
35

BREAD HEAD

Kittiwat Unarrom makes edible human heads and torsos out of dough! His workplace looks like a mortuary or a serial killer's dungeon, but it is in fact a bakery.

Visitors to Unarrom's workshop near Bangkok are alarmed to see the heads and torsos lined up on shelves, and rows of arms and hands hanging from meat hooks. The Thai art student, whose family runs a bakery, uses anatomy books and his memories of visiting a forensics museum to create the human body parts. In addition to heads crafted from bread, chocolate, raisins, and cashews, he makes human arms and feet, and chicken and pig parts, incorporating red food coloring for extra bloody effect. "When people see the bread, they don't want to eat it," he says. "But when they taste it, it's just normal bread. The lesson is, don't judge by appearances."

His macabre project started out as the centerpiece of his final dissertation for his Master of Arts degree, but as word spread about his novelty-shaped bread, regular orders began coming in from the curious or from pranksters who want to surprise their friends.

Basing the models on pictures from anatomy books, Thai art student Kittiwat Unarrom lovingly creates lifelike human heads from bread. Not surprisingly, most people think twice before eating the heads.

When customers first saw Kittiwat's room of realistic-looking human body parts, they were shocked and thought he was crazy.

Some of Kittiwat's creations are really gruesome and would not look out of place in a chamber of horrors. And if they're not bloody enough, he adds red food coloring to increase the effect.

LET IT BE

This toilet paper, auctioned at a starting price of £40,000 ($71,000), was removed from the toilets in the EMI studios at Abbey Road, London, England, when the Beatles refused to use it, objecting to its hardness and shininess. They were also said to have disliked the fact that EMI was stamped on every sheet.

and such weird exhibits as Octopus Girl! The museum and nightclub is run by Carl Crew and Robert Ferguson, who collect circus memorabilia.

BEARDED LADY
Vivian Wheeler has a weird claim to fame—she is the woman with the world's longest beard. Wheeler, who comes from Wood River, Illinois, was born with facial hair, having inherited a genetic hormonal disorder from her mother. Her father refused to accept her beard and forced her to shave it off from the age of seven, but she later traveled with sideshow acts under the stage name of Melinda Maxie, dying her natural red hair black for greater impact. Her full beard has now reached a length of 11 in (28 cm), although she usually wears it tied up.

SELF-LIPOSUCTION
Believe it or not, Yugoslav-born plastic surgeon Dimitrije Panfilov performed liposuction on himself to remove his double chin!

TINY LETTERS
In 2004, physicists at Boston College, Massachussetts, managed to carve minuscule letters into a single strand of human hair. Using a laser, they created letters that were 15 micrometers tall. The technique can form items a thousand times smaller than the diameter of a human hair.

MIRACLE BIRTH
Nhlahla Cwayita was born healthy at Cape Town, South Africa, in 2003, despite developing in her mother's liver. She was only the fourth baby in the world to survive such a pregnancy.

CIRCUS CLUB
At one of the world's strangest nightclubs, the California Institute of Abnormalarts, you can dance the night away in the company of the remains of a dead clown, the stuffed carcass of a piglet-Chihuahua hybrid, a mummified arm,

BEAD ART
Liza Lou of Topanga, California, used 40 million glass beads to create a kitchen and garden that was first displayed at the Kemper Museum of

ON A SHOESTRING

Big Bear City, California, is home to The Shoe Tree—no one quite knows how it started, but the tree continues to accumulate shoe upon shoe. Local police tried to prevent the tree being used in this way by removing all the shoes and fencing off the area, but by the next morning it was covered once again.

Contemporary Art in Kansas City in 1998. If the beads had been strung together, they would have stretched about 380 mi (610 km), the same distance as that between Los Angeles and San Francisco.

HOT STUFF

New Mexico State University has developed a special Halloween chili pepper, a miniature ornamental specimen that changes from black to orange. However,

Paul Bosland, head of the university's chili-breeding program, warns that these hot peppers are actually too hot to eat.

BIRD POOP

An American firm offers individually crafted models of birds made from genuine Californian horse dung!

FAKING FOR FUN

Chaucey Shea, of St. Catherine's, Ontario, Canada, has a potentially illegal hobby. He has mastered more than 2,000 forgeries of famous signatures, including English playwright William Shakespeare, and several presidents of the United States.

SEAT OF LEARNING

Bill Jarrett, a retired artist from Grand Rapids, Michigan, has been studying toilet paper for the past 30 years and now boasts a vast collection of tissue-related memorabilia.

TWO-FACED KITTEN

A kitten was born in Glide, Oregon, in June 2005, with two faces! Gemini astounded vets and owner Lee Bluetear with her two mouths, two tongues, two noses, and four eyes. Sadly, she died within a week.

SENTIMENTAL VALUE

Ezekiel Rubottom decided to keep his left foot after it was amputated in 2005! He stored it in the front porch of his Kansas home. After neigbors complained, he said "I'm not sick, I just wanted my foot."

WACKY WEDDING

At a wedding in Calgary, Alberta, Canada, in 1998, the bride was a sword swallower, the groom tamed bees, and the maid of honor made a living eating live bugs and worms! Megan Evans married Jim Rogers (Calgary's "Bee Man") in front of 200 musicians and freak-show performers, including worm-loving bridesmaid Brenda Fox.

SPLAT EXPERT

Mark Hostetler, an ecologist at the University of Florida, has written a book on how to identify insect splats left on your car. The book is titled *That Gunk On Your Car*.

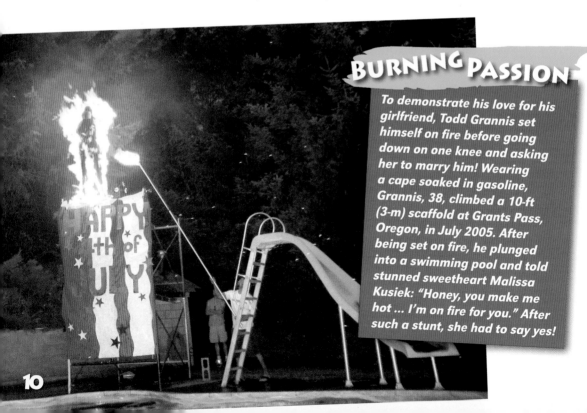

BURNING PASSION

To demonstrate his love for his girlfriend, Todd Grannis set himself on fire before going down on one knee and asking her to marry him! Wearing a cape soaked in gasoline, Grannis, 38, climbed a 10-ft (3-m) scaffold at Grants Pass, Oregon, in July 2005. After being set on fire, he plunged into a swimming pool and told stunned sweetheart Malissa Kusiek: "Honey, you make me hot ... I'm on fire for you." After such a stunt, she had to say yes!

HALF-SIZE JEANIE

Born without any legs, Jeanie Tomaini achieved fame in U.S. sideshows as "The Half Girl." While on tour, Jeanie, who is 2 ft 6 in (0.76 m), married Al, who stood 8 ft 4 in (2.54 m) tall and wore size 22 shoes. They went on to form a successful act as "The World's Strangest Couple."

OPEN
WIDE

IN DEPTH

Jim Mouth, is a comedy entertainer based in Las Vegas who has been performing incredible stunts for more than 20 years. These often involve putting absolutely anything in his mouth!

When did you get started—and why do you keep going?
"My first stunt, when I was about 29, was playing drums for two weeks non stop. I had to drink lots of coffee to stay awake! My comedy shows are more of a full-time thing, but my biggest drive is to use stunts to raise money for charity."

What is your most famous stunt?
"I like doing the "most cigarettes in the mouth" stunt. I'm up to 159 cigarettes now. I've performed this on TV many times. I put all the cigarettes in apart from one which the host of the show puts in. Then they light them with two propane torches, I cough and wheeze for about three minutes, then spit them out. I'm dizzy for about half an hour afterward. One time I coughed out about 100 cigarettes—the crazy thing is I'm actually a non-smoker. I've actually done this stunt on non-smoking days to support people giving up cigarettes."

Do you have a special technique?
"Before a stunt I wedge corks into my mouth to stretch my lips, but my real secret is that I can dislocate my jaw. I didn't know I was doing it until they X-rayed me on a TV show last year. All I knew was that it was painful and made my eyes water!"

What other stunts do you do?
"Mouth stunts include smoking 41 cigars at once, and 41 pipes. We once had a whole band playing music under the water in a pool, and and another time I sat on every seat in the University of Michigan football stadium, the biggest in the U.S.A. There were 101,701 seats—it took me 96 hours 12 minutes, and four pairs of pants!"

How dangerous are your stunts?
"Apparently when my jaw dislocates it rests on my larynx, which could suffocate me. No one will insure me!"

Is there anything you would not do?
"Because I play drums I really don't want to break a finger or an arm. But I will put up with anything in my mouth—I might try keeping a tarantula spider in my mouth for half an hour."

How long will you carry on?
"My goal is to do one stunt every year for at least the next ten years. One I've got in the pipeline is "most hats on the head"—I'm aiming for a stack of 300, which will be about 8½ ft tall and weigh about 110 lb. I'll probably retire when I'm in my sixties—I'll do 170 cigarettes and then call it a day."

ASH ART

Bettye Jane Brokl incorporates the ashes of dead people into abstract paintings. The Biloxi, Mississippi, artist sprinkles the cremation ashes on the artwork to create a pictorial memorial for a loved one.

GERBIL INSTALLATION

An artist from Newcastle, England, made her pet gerbil the star of a 2005 exhibition. "The Gerbil's Guide to the Galaxy" showed Sally Madge's rodent chewing its way through a 1933 edition of the *New Illustrated Universal Reference Book*, "choosing" certain words to eat.

FIBERGLASS SHELL

A mud turtle that had its shell broken into eight pieces by cars in Lutz, Florida, was given a new fiberglass one in 1982.

JUNK EXHIBITION

In 2005, an exhibition in London, England, by Japanese artist Tomoko Takahashi featured 7,600 pieces of junk. The exhibits included old washing machines, broken toys, a rusty muck-spreader, and three stuffed blackbirds.

LOVE SHACK

In April 2005, a building was covered in 6,000 love letters, some penned by international celebrities, as part of the annual Auckland Festival in New Zealand.

MIND READER

Matthew Nagle, of Weymouth, Massachusetts, has a brain chip that reads his mind. Severely paralyzed after being stabbed in the neck in 2001, he has a revolutionary implant that enables him to control everyday objects simply by thinking about them. After drilling a hole into his head, surgeons implanted the chip a millimeter deep into his brain. Wafer-thin electrodes attached to the chip detect the electrical signals generated by his thoughts and relay them through wires into a computer. The brain signals are analyzed by the computer and translated into cursor movements. As well as operating a computer, software linked to other items in the room allows him to think his TV on and off and change channels.

SOARING SUCCESS

For her 1999 work "100 Ideas in the Atmosphere," Canadian performance artist Marie-Suzanne Désilets launched 100 helium balloons from the rooftop of a Montreal shopping mall with self-addressed notecards and an invitation to reply.

SLOW DINING

There's no fast food at June, a new restaurant in Lakewood Ranch, Florida. The nine-course meals take four hours to eat.

HEAD REATTACHED

Marcos Parra must be one of the luckiest guys alive. He survived a horrific car crash in 2002, in which his head was technically severed from the rest of his body. His skull was torn from his cervical spine, leaving his head detached from his neck. Only skin and his spinal cord kept the two body parts connected. Amazingly, however, surgeons in Phoenix, Arizona, managed to reattach his head. The bones were pulled into the right position by two screws placed at the back of his neck, enabling Parra to live.

MIRACLE HEART

Nikolai Mikhalnichuk leads a healthy life even though his heart stopped beating several years ago. He suffered a heart attack when his wife said she was leaving him, but doctors in Saratov, Russia, found that although his heart has stopped, its blood vessels are able to keep on pumping blood around his body.

BUSHY BROWS

In 2004, Frank Ames, of Saranac, New York State, had his eyebrow hair measured at an incredible 3.1 in (7.8 cm) long. Ames said "I don't know why it grows like that. It just always has."

EXTRA DIGITS

Filipinos Albert M. Perculeza and his son Karl Cedric each have 12 digits on their hands and 12 digits on their feet (see below). All 48 digits are fully functional.

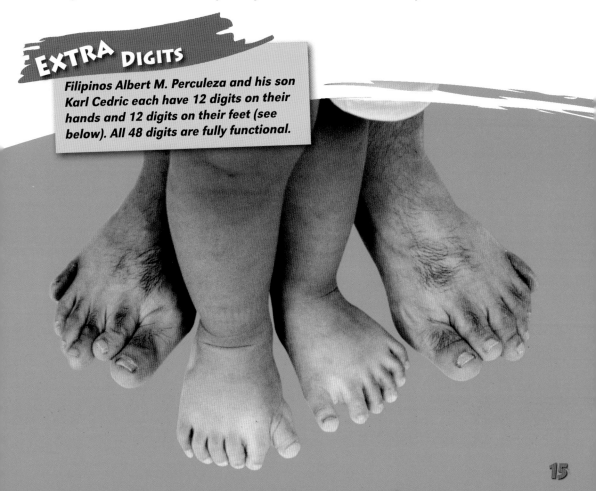

HUMAN SOAP

A bar of soap that was said to have been made from body fat pumped from the Italian Prime Minister Silvio Berlusconi sold for almost $20,000 in 2005. Artist Gianni Motti said that he acquired the fat from a private Swiss clinic where Berlusconi reportedly underwent liposuction. Motti said the fat was "jelly-like and stunk horribly."

HAM ACTORS

Father and son, Olivier and Yohann Roussel, won one of Europe's most coveted prizes in 2005—the French Pig-squealing Championships. Dressed in pig outfits, the Roussels impressed the judges and spectators with squeals, grunts, and snuffles to represent the four key stages of a pig's life—birth, suckling, mating, and death under the knife.

BLIND DIAGNOSIS

Dr. James T. Clack, of Wadley, Alabama, treated patients in the 1940s even though he was blind.

HARDY EATER

"Hungry" Charles Hardy, of Brooklyn, New York, describes himself as "the Michael Jordan of competitive eating." In 2001, he ate 23 hot dogs in 12 minutes, and also became Matzo Ball Eating world champion. But his talent has drawbacks. Hardy explains: "I found a place in Manhattan with all-you-can-eat sushi for $19.95. When the lady sees me coming, she hits the clock and gives me one and a half hours."

HEART BEAT

Jeweler Didier Verhill, of Antwerp, Belgium, creates wedding rings engraved with the couple's heartbeat pattern taken from a cardiograph!

SNEEZY PLATE

Allergist Dr. Edwin Dombrowski, of Stamford, Connecticut, had the automobile licence plate "AH-CHoo."

ZERO INFLATION

Dr. Anna Perkins, of Westerloo, New York, charged the same rates in 1993 that she had set in 1928: $4 for an office visit, $5 for a house call, and $25 to deliver a baby.

SELL-OUT FUNERAL

When Dr. William Price, of Llantrisant, south Wales, died in 1893, more than 6,000 tickets were sold for his public cremation, as specified in his will.

BUTTON KING

Dalton Stevens, of Hartsville, South Carolina, has fixed an incredible 600,000 buttons to his Pontiac hearse. Another 60,000 buttons cover the coffin inside! Besides the hearse, he has shoes, musical instruments, and even a toilet covered with buttons.

WRIST-BREAKER

That K.S. Raghavendra, from India, is capable of breaking 13 eggs in 30 seconds doesn't sound amazing in itself, except he doesn't break them by clenching his fist, but by bending his hand back over his wrist.

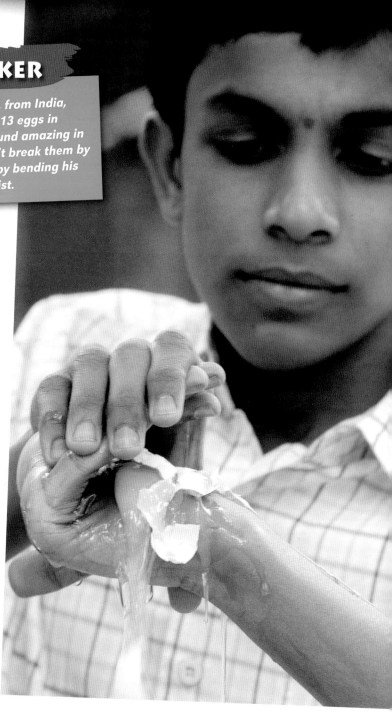

TOBACCO MOUTH

Prince Randian, known as "The Living Torso," had no arms or legs. However, he amazingly learned to roll, light, and smoke a cigarette by moving his mouth.

FOUR-LEGGED WOMAN

Myrtle Corbin, the four-legged woman from Texas, had a malformed Siamese twin, which resulted in Myrtle having two pairs of legs. She used to gallop across the stage like a horse.

SNOWBALL FLAG

In 1998, Vasili Mochanou, of Ottawa, Ontario, created a replica of the Canadian Flag using 27,000 snowballs!

TWO-SIDED

Edward Mordrake was born a Siamese twin, and had another face on the reverse of his—that of a beautiful girl whose eyes used to follow you around the room.

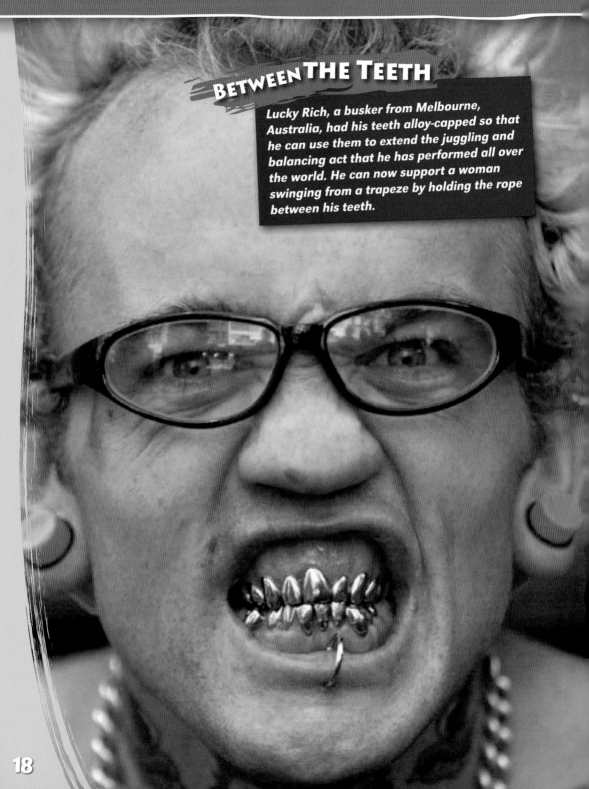

BETWEEN THE TEETH

Lucky Rich, a busker from Melbourne, Australia, had his teeth alloy-capped so that he can use them to extend the juggling and balancing act that he has performed all over the world. He can now support a woman swinging from a trapeze by holding the rope between his teeth.

FREE PIG

In an unusual bid to boost sales in 2005, an entrepreneurial British housing developer offered a free gift of a live pig to anyone who bought a property from him. Jeremy Paxton, who is based in Gloucestershire, England, promised that the rare breed Gloucester Old Spot pigs would be fully house-trained before delivery.

GIANT RODENT

For a 2004 art festival, Dutchman Florentun Hofman built a sculpture of a beaver 100 ft (31 m) long and 25 ft (8 m) high, using just wood and reeds. The year before, he created a 37-ft (11-m) high rabbit.

NOSE GROWN

Madina Yusuf had her face reconstructed by growing a new nose on her arm. The Nigerian woman was severely disfigured by a flesh-eating disease that left her without a nose and with very little mouth. But, in 2001, she flew to Aberdeen, Scotland, where Dr. Peter Ayliffe grafted her new nose from extra skin grown on her arm, plus bone and cartilage that had been taken from her right rib.

ASTRAL GROOMING

Astronauts in space shave using razors equipped with tiny vacuum cleaners inside!

BALLOON SCULPTURE

U.S. balloon sculptor Larry Moss used more than 40,000 balloons to construct a model of two football players at Mol, Belgium, in 2000. Each player was 40 ft (12 m) tall.

THE SMELL OF ITALY

In 2003, Ducio Cresci, of Florence, Italy, created a series of bathroom products— including soap, lotion, and bubble bath—that smelled just like pizza!

TINY TACKLER

The ace defence tackler on the football team at Flint Southwestern Academy High School, Michigan, was only 3 ft (0.9 m) tall, having been left with no legs after a 1994 railroad accident. Willie McQueen earned his place on the team by courage and tenacity. He didn't play in a wheelchair or wear prostheses, but scooted around to create havoc in the opposing backfield.

GARBAGE TOUR

In Chicago in 2005, people were paying $7 to see some of the city's less desirable spots on a three-hour bus tour of garbage sites, landfills, and smelly sludge sewage fields. The excursion showed residents and visitors what happens to garbage once it leaves their trash cans.

LOBSTER FEET

The fingers of this unidentified man from upstate western New York have mutated to look like lobster claws. This was the result of inbreeding.

ELASTIC MAN

Dubbed "Mr Elastic," Moses Lanham can turn his feet around 180 degrees, completely backwards, and then walk in the opposite direction!

Lanham puts his unique talent down to being born with extra ligaments and cartilage within the joints of his ankles, knees, and hips, which enable him to rotate his bones freely within the sockets of his joints.

Amazingly, he didn't realize he had this ability until he suffered a fall in gym class at the age of 14 and landed awkwardly. Jumping to his feet, he suddenly found that he could easily twist both of his feet around backward. Lanham, from Monroe, Michigan, has discovered that his son Trey also appears to have inherited the extra joint tissue. At 11, he can turn his feet backward just like his dad! "He can't walk backwards yet," says Moses, "but he is learning."

Moses enjoys putting his best foot backwards, and often performs at local fund-raising events.

Moses Lanham's body contains extra joint tissue that enables him to turn his feet backwards. Moses can even walk backwards too!

OUR LADY OF THE UNDERPASS

Thousands of worshipers flocked to a Chicago underpass in April 2005 and created a shrine of candles and flowers, after a watery mark on the concrete wall was interpreted as an image of the Virgin Mary. Visitors touched and kissed the mark, which was thought to have been caused by salt running down from the Kennedy Expressway overhead. However, the devout insisted it was a miracle that had appeared in order to mark the death of Pope John Paul II.

LEDGER BALANCING

Balancing ledgers while balancing on ledges or deep-sea diving with a tax return are just some ways to perform Extreme Accounting. First established by Arnold Chiswick, the extreme sport incorporates everything involved in an accounting desk job with the added thrill of sporting action.

SPECIES FOR SALE

A new species of rodent was discovered in 2005—for sale on a food stall in a market in Laos. The rock rat, or kha-nyou, was spotted by conservation biologist Robert Timmins who knew it was something he'd never seen before. The animal looks like a cross between a rat and a squirrel, but is not actually related to any other rodents at all.

SNAKE DIET

Neeranjan Bhaskar claims to have eaten more than 4,000 snakes, including deadly cobras. Bhaskar, who is otherwise vegetarian, hunts for snakes every morning on the banks of the Ghagra River near his home in India. He first ate a snake at the age of seven.

SKIN HORROR

After being prescribed a common antibiotic to treat a routine sinus infection in 2003, Sarah Yeargain, from San Diego, California, looked on in horror as her skin began peeling away in sheets. With Sarah's condition—caused by a severe allergic reaction to the drug—getting worse, more of her skin came off in her mother's hands as she was carried into a hospital. She eventually lost the skin from her entire body—including her internal organs and the membranes covering her mouth, throat, and eyes. Doctors gave her no chance of survival, but they covered her body in an artificial skin replacement and within a few days her own skin returned.

DOG DIVER

When Dwane Folsom went scuba diving, his dog went too! Folsom, from Boynton Beach, Florida, designed the first scuba-diving outfit for dogs, comprising a lead-weighted jacket, a helmet, and a tube that allowed the animal to draw air from the human diver's tank. Folsom and his dog, named Shadow, regularly dived to depths of 13 ft (4 m).

HOLY SHOWER

In 2005, Jeffrey Rigo, of Pittsburgh, Pennsylvania, sold a water stain on his bathroom wall for nearly $2,000 because he considered that it bore a resemblance to Jesus. Following the publicity for the "Shower Jesus," Rigo had requests from people who wanted to pray in his bathtub.

HIDDEN MONKEYS

When Californian Robert Cusack was asked if he had anything to declare on arrival at Los Angeles Airport in 2002, customs officers could hardly have expected what they would find. They discovered a pair of pygmy monkeys in his pants and a bird of paradise in his suitcase. Cusack was subsequently sentenced to 57 days in jail for smuggling the monkeys, as well as four exotic birds, and 50 rare orchids into the U.S. all the way from Thailand.

GREAT BALLS OF FIRE!

Stonehenge in Wiltshire, England, was the location for a massive synchronized fire-eating spectacular. Seventy fire-eaters came together to create a landscape of flames at the event in September 2004.

EMERGENCY REPAIRS

Jonas Scott, from Salt Lake City, Utah, was left with no esophagus after industrial cleaning fluid at his workplace ate away his insides in 1988. With no stomach, he had to be fed intravenously. He went three years without eating solids until surgeons connected the remaining 7 ft (2.1 m) of his small intestine directly to the base of his throat so that he could eat almost normally again.

AMBIDEXTROUS BILINGUIST

In 2004, Amanullah, a 53-year-old man from India, learned to write different sentences simultaneously with both hands. Most amazing of all, he could write one sentence in English, and the other in Tamil.

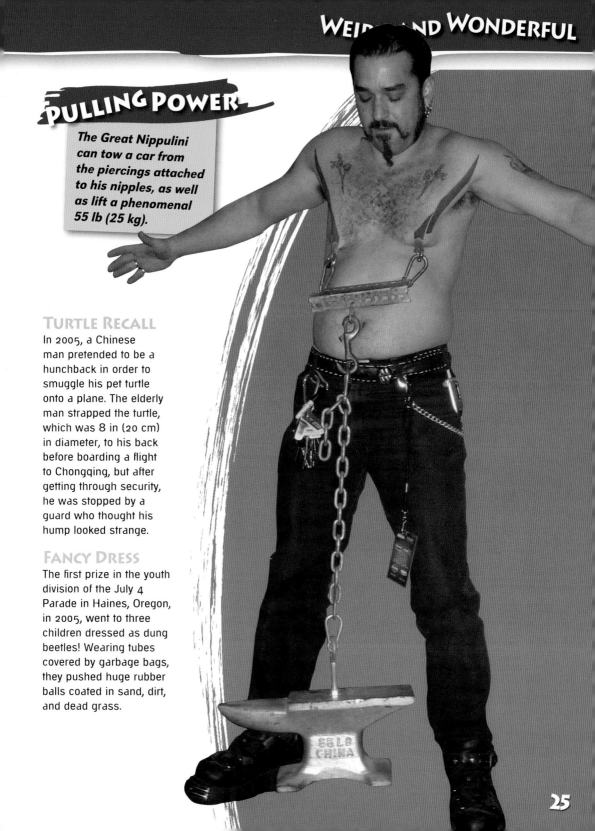

PULLING POWER

The Great Nippulini can tow a car from the piercings attached to his nipples, as well as lift a phenomenal 55 lb (25 kg).

TURTLE RECALL

In 2005, a Chinese man pretended to be a hunchback in order to smuggle his pet turtle onto a plane. The elderly man strapped the turtle, which was 8 in (20 cm) in diameter, to his back before boarding a flight to Chongqing, but after getting through security, he was stopped by a guard who thought his hump looked strange.

FANCY DRESS

The first prize in the youth division of the July 4 Parade in Haines, Oregon, in 2005, went to three children dressed as dung beetles! Wearing tubes covered by garbage bags, they pushed huge rubber balls coated in sand, dirt, and dead grass.

LIVE BY THE SWORD

New Yorker Natasha Veruschka, claims to be the world's only belly-dancing sword swallower, and defies a strict religious upbringing to risk her life for her passion.

When did you first become fascinated by swords?
"My British mother died when I was two. I don't remember my Siberian father—I was adopted into a strict Mennonite family in southern Ukraine. I wasn't allowed to hear music, or look in a mirror, or cut my hair. When I was four I saw a knife in a church—I was mesmerized. I remember putting the tip of it on my tongue to feel it."

How did your act begin?
"I grew up in countries including India, Egypt, and Iran, and later took belly dancing lessons in New York. I learned sword balancing, but one night I ended a performance by kissing the sword—I realized then that I wanted to be a sword swallower. The first time I did it, nine years ago, it felt like home—it made me complete."

What kinds of swords do you swallow?
"The longest is 27½ inches—which is a lot because I am only 5 ft 4 in tall and weigh just over 100 lb. I have 25 different swords—including a Sai sword, which is an eight-sided Japanese war weapon. I can swallow up to 13 swords at once."

Which is the most dangerous?
"The neon sword, which is filled with poisonous gas and is so fragile that your stomach muscles can shatter it inside you. It is electric and heats up—one time, it started to burn and adhere to my insides. Since 1942, six people have died swallowing one."

Have you ever cut yourself on a sword?
"Once I nearly died—I lost 53 per cent of my blood. I had three swords inside me and a man pushed me. The blades scissored and cut my lower esophagus. After the show, I was vomiting blood everywhere and even had a near-death experience. They told me at the hospital that I would be in the morgue by the following morning. I was back swallowing swords within a month."

Where does the sword go?
"To the bottom of the stomach. I can swallow a chocolate cherry, put a sword down, and bring it back up. You have to overcome much more than a gag reflex—the sword has to go past two muscle sphincters as well, on its way past the lungs and heart."

Do you have any special techniques?
"I say a prayer before every performance, and use yoga to go into 'a zone.' I use no lubricant, no special tubes. You need a lot of upper body strength—the swords weigh close to 12½ lb when I swallow them all at once—and a lot of lung capacity. It's not magic. I have been X-rayed and you can see the sword in me. The neon one glows through my body for all to see."

What drives you—and how long will you do this?
"My family have shunned me for what I do. To them, I am dead. I think this all stems from an 'I'll show you' attitude. As for how long, I won't be happy until I'm the oldest female belly-dancing sword swallower in the world!"

MINI COWS

In an attempt to combat his country's serious milk shortage of 1987, Fidel Castro urged his scientists to create a breed of mini cows. Castro wanted the most productive cows cloned and shrunk to the size of dogs so that families could keep one inside their apartments. There, the cows would feed on grass grown under fluorescent lights.

PECULIAR PASTIMES

In Rieti, Italy, there is an annual washtub race in which contestants race wooden washtubs along a course 875 yd (800 m) long.

EXTREME CARVING

In Port Elgin, Ontario, Canada, there is an annual pumpkin festival that includes such unique events as underwater pumpkin carving.

BUSSE LOAD

When the Busse family marked the 150th anniversary of the arrival of their ancestors in the U.S.A. from Germany, it was no ordinary reunion: 2,369 family members turned up at Grayslake, Illinois, in 1998, some from as far away as Africa.

COMPETITIVE KITE-FLYING

Kite fighting is common at the spring Festival of Basant in Lahore, Pakistan. Skilled kite-flyers from all around the country use bladed and chemical-lined strings to bring down or capture their opponents' kites.

SPACE ODDITY

Canadian performance artist Julie Andrée T. sought to redefine space by walking blindfold in a confined space for six hours, marking the walls and singing a children's song.

TWO NOSES

Bill Durks was born in 1913 with two noses, each with a single nostril. Between the bridges of his noses, he painted a third eye, over what may have been a vestigial eye socket, and became known in U.S. sideshows as "The Man with Three Eyes." He married Milly Durks, "The Alligator-skinned Woman From New Jersey."

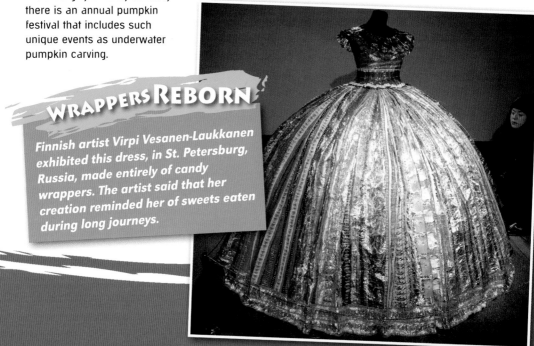

WRAPPERS REBORN

Finnish artist Virpi Vesanen-Laukkanen exhibited this dress, in St. Petersburg, Russia, made entirely of candy wrappers. The artist said that her creation reminded her of sweets eaten during long journeys.

HUGE HALLOWEEN

Belgian artist Michel Dircken sits in his carving, created during a competition for the fastest carving of a jack o'lantern in October 2005. The pumpkin weighed 637 lb (289 kg) and measured 131 in (333 cm) around.

BIRTH ART

As part of an exhibition in a German art gallery, a woman gave birth in front of dozens of spectators. Ramune Gele had the baby girl, named Audra, in 2005, at the DNA gallery in Berlin. The father, Winfried Witt, called the experience "an existential work of art."

TOE THUMB

After Peter Morris, from Kingswinford, England, lost his thumb in a 1993 accident, doctors replaced it with his big toe.

SEWN EAR

Trampled by a bull in 1993, Jim McManus, of Calgary, Canada, had his left ear reattached by doctors—aided by 75 leeches to help control the bleeding.

FYRE EATER

Eating fire, swallowing swords, juggling machetes, hammering nails up his own nose—they're all in a day's work for the Amazing Blazing Tyler Fyre!

Fyre (real name Tyler Fleet), born in Georgia, was a one-off even as a kid, when he found that he could squirt milk, water, and even spaghetti and meatballs out of his nose. He learned trapeze, juggling, balancing, the high wire, and fire-eating, before progressing to a routine as a Human Blockhead. In ten years, Fyre, who also eats glass, razor blades, live crickets, and lit cigarettes, and has been known to pound a nail through a hole in his tongue, has done more than 7,500 live shows, sometimes performing 15 a day. He admits: "It's grueling on the body. At the Coney Island Circus Sideshow I was the Human Blockhead, the sword swallower, I ate fire, and I did the inverted escape act, cranked up by my ankles until my head was 6 ft above the stage."

When it comes to swallowing swords, Tyler's act puts him at the cutting edge of show business.

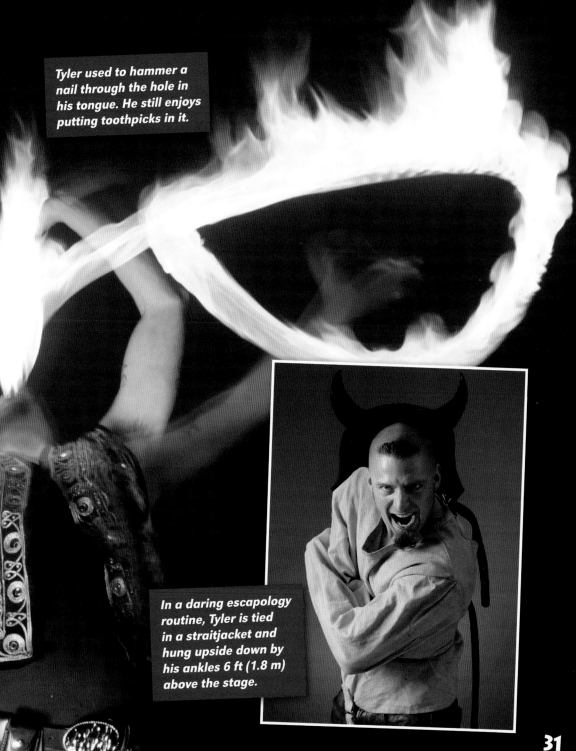

Tyler used to hammer a nail through the hole in his tongue. He still enjoys putting toothpicks in it.

In a daring escapology routine, Tyler is tied in a straitjacket and hung upside down by his ankles 6 ft (1.8 m) above the stage.

THROUGH THE NOSE

Jin Guolong, from China, can drink through his nose—he consumes both milk and alcohol using this method.

KILLER TREE

In 1860, nearly 200 years after his death, the Rhode Island Historical Society exhumed the body of Roger Williams—only to find that he had been eaten by an apple tree! The coffin was empty apart from the invading tree roots. A large root curved where his head should have been and entered the chest cavity before growing down the spine. It then branched at the two legs and upturned into feet.

ICE SCULPTOR

Richard Bubin, aged 44, from Wilkins, Pennsylvania, has been sculpting ice for more than 20 years and once carved 61 blocks in under 4½ hours.

For Pittsburgh's First Night celebration in January 2005, he turned ten giant blocks of ice into a sculpture of the Roberto Clemente Bridge.

JUMBO JUNK

British artist Anthony Heywood made a full-size elephant sculpture in 2004 entirely from household junk, including TV sets, heaters, fans, radios, and a toilet.

STAIR RIDE

In the 2005 urban Down the Hill bike race, held in the town of Taxco, Mexico, competitors rode their mountain bikes through a house! They went in through a door, down a flight of stairs and exited through another door. They also sped through narrow alleys and jumped heights of 13 ft (4 m) on the 2-mi (3.2-km) course.

LEGGED IT!

A man testing an artificial leg worth $17,000 ran off without paying the bill. The theft occurred after the man called in to collect a prosthetic from a specialist in Des Moines, Iowa, in 2005, and was allowed to take it away for a couple of hours to ensure that it fitted him properly.

CHICKEN PROTEST

Ottawa performance artist Rob Thompson caged a man and a woman in 1997 to protest about the conditions of commercially bred chickens. Eric Wolf and Pam Meldrum spent a week together in the small wooden cage to make the point. Their drinking water came from a dripping hose and they ate vegetarian mash.

LOVE BIRDS

During the Middle Ages, people in Europe are said to have believed that birds chose their mates every year on Valentine's Day!

X-RAY EYES

A teenage Russian girl appears to have X-ray vision, which enables her to see inside human bodies. Natalia Demkina has baffled scientists across the world by describing the insides of bodies in detail and using her talent to correctly diagnose the medical conditions of complete strangers. She says that she possesses dual vision when looking at others, but that she can't see inside her own body. Natalia switches from normal to X-ray vision by focusing on a person for two minutes.

PRETTY AS A PICTURE

A participant in the
13th International Tattoo
Convention, held in
Frankfurt, Germany, in
2005, sports a tattoo on
the back of his head.

MINI MARRIAGE

In 1863, "General Tom Thumb," or Charles Stratton, married Lavinia Warren. Lavinia was heralded as a miniature of perfect proportions, and the marriage was a major event in New York society.

PET PILLOWS

In 2005, Nevada taxidermist Jeanette Hall offered to make fur pillows from dead pets. Each Pet Pillow was handmade for prices ranging from $65 for a cat to $150 for a horse. Hall described the idea as a "unique way of keeping your pets close to you even after they pass away."

CRICKET LOVER

Danny Capps, of Madison, Wisconsin, spits dead crickets from his mouth over distances of up to 30 ft (9 m). Capps, who has been fascinated by insects since he was a small boy, says that dead crickets have no flavor.

SHOPPING BREAK

Tired shoppers in Minnesota's Mall of America can rest their weary legs for 70 cents a minute. In the Bloomington shopping center there is a store called MinneNAPolis aimed at bored spouses of shoppers and also at travelers, who need a nap after a lengthy flight, but aren't staying long enough to book a hotel.

PAVEMENT PICASSO

Ben Wilson roams the streets of London, England, looking for used chewing gum, which he turns into works of art. He burns the gum with a blowtorch, adds a clear enamel as a base, then colors in acrylic enamels, and finishes with a coat of varnish. His gum gallery includes human portraits, animals, and buildings.

PREGNANT BOY

When seven-year-old Alamjan Nematilaev's tummy began to bulge, his parents thought he had rickets, a common childhood disease in his native Kazakhstan. But, in 2003, a concerned schoolteacher took him to hospital, where doctors removed a 4-lb (1.8-kg) baby boy from Alamjan's stomach! Alamjan had been born with the fetus of his twin brother growing inside him. For seven years it had lived like a parasite, growing a head, a body, hair, and nails. Doctors were able to save Alamjan but not the 8-in (20-cm) fetus.

WALL EATER

In 2005, Emily Katrencik ate through the wall of her Brooklyn gallery until she could put her head through it—all in the name of art. She said: "The wall has a mild flavor. The texture is more prominent than the taste—it's chalky with tiny sharp pieces in it." Visitors to the gallery could eat bread made with minerals extracted from the wall.

FROG BIRTH

A woman from Iran was reported to have given birth to a gray frog-like creature in 2004. It apparently grew from a larva that had entered the woman as she swam in a dirty pool. A doctor described the creature as resembling a frog in appearance, particularly the shape of the fingers, and the size and shape of the tongue.

IN FOND MEMORY

Swedish artist and sculptor Lars Widenfalk has created a violin with a difference. He sculpted the working instrument from the tombstone of his late grandfather, Gustav. The violin's fingerboard, pegs, tailpiece, and chin rest are all made of ebony, and by lining the interior with real gold, it produces the finest possible tone. The instrument is considered to be worth in the region of $1.7 million.

TALON CONTEST

Louise Hollis, of Compton, California, has let her toenails grow to a staggering 6 in (15 cm) long. She has to wear open-toed shoes with at least 3-in (7.6-cm) soles to stop her nails dragging along the ground, and she needs 2½ bottles of nail polish to paint the nails on both her hands and feet.

PAN CHRIST

As Juan Pastrano, of Prairie Lea, Texas, was hanging up his frying pan after washing it in 2005, he spotted an uncanny image where the anti-stick coating on the pan had worn thin. There before him was the face of Jesus Christ in a crown of thorns. He promptly sealed the pan in a plastic bag to protect the image from curious visitors.

TOOTHY FOOT

Teenager Doug Pritchard, of Lenoir, North Carolina, went to his doctor in 1978 with a sore foot. Amazingly a tooth was found growing in the bottom of his instep!

THORNY LANDING

Jens Jenson, of Denmark, fell into a pile of spiky barberries in 1990 and had to visit his doctor 248 times to have a total of 32,131 thorns removed from his punctured body.

SMALL WONDER

Ma Chaoqin, from China, is 22 years old, but still looks like a baby. She suffers from an incurable disease called Rachitic, or rickets, and as a result has failed to grow at a normal rate.

HEARING IN COLORS

Color-blind art student Neil Harbisson wears a special device that enables him to "hear" colors.

Neil, from Spain, uses a device called the Eye-Borg, that was invented by Adam Montandon, a digital multimedia expert from Plymouth, England. It works by converting light waves into sounds, and consists of a digital camera and a backpack that contains the computer and headset for Neil to listen to the colors. A low-pitched sound indicates reds, a high-pitched sound indicates violet, while shades of blue and green fall somewhere in between.

Now Neil, who takes off the invention only when he sleeps, is able to buy clothes that he "likes the sound of." He can also order his favorite foods, whereas previously he struggled to differentiate between apple juice and orange juice.

When Neil first applied for a passport and sent a photo of himself wearing the camera, it was rejected. "So I sent a letter to the passport office explaining that I was a cyborg. They accepted me as a cyborg."

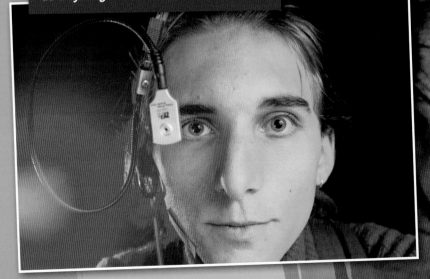

Neil now paints in vibrant colors.

SNAKE MAN

For more than 50 years, Bill Haast injected himself with deadly snake venom. He built up such powerful antibodies in his system that his blood was used as a snakebite antidote. Haast, who ran a Florida serpentarium, began in 1948 with tiny amounts of rattlesnake venom and built up the dosage until, by the time he was 90, he was injecting himself once a week with venom from 32 species. Although he was bitten more than 180 times by snakes from which a few drops of venom could kill any ordinary human, Haast managed to survive every single time.

TWO HEARTS

A boy in Tbilisi, Georgia, was born with two hearts. In 2004, doctors discovered that one-year-old Goga Diasamidze had been born with a second perfectly functioning heart near his stomach.

SNAIL TRAIL

In Januray 2005, Chilean artist Paola Podesta promoted her new exhibition by gluing 2,000 plastic snails to a Santiago church. The snail trail led from the Church of Santo Expedito to the nearby Codar art gallery.

OMELET SURPRISE

When Ursula Beckley, of Long Island, New York, was preparing an omelette in 1989, she cracked open an egg— only to see a 6-in (15-cm) black snake slither out. She sued her local supermarket for $3.6 million on the grounds that she was so traumatized by the incident that she could never look at an egg again.

POOPER SCOOPER

Steve Relles makes a living by scooping up dog poop! The Delmar Dog Butler, as he calls himself, has more than 100 clients in New York State who pay $10, each for a weekly clean of their yard.

ROBOT RIDERS

In 2005, Qatar, in the Middle East, staged a spectacular camel race using robot jockeys. Seven robots were placed on top of seven camels at Al Shahaniyya racecourse, near the country's capital Doha, after there had been widespread protests about the use of children as jockeys in the popular sport.

SENSITIVE SHIRT

Italian designer Francesca Rosella has come up with the perfect gift for people involved in long-distance relationships—a hugging T-shirt. Fitted with sensors, the T-shirt simulates the missing partner's caress by recreating breath, touch, and heartbeat based on information transmitted to the T-shirt via their cell phone.

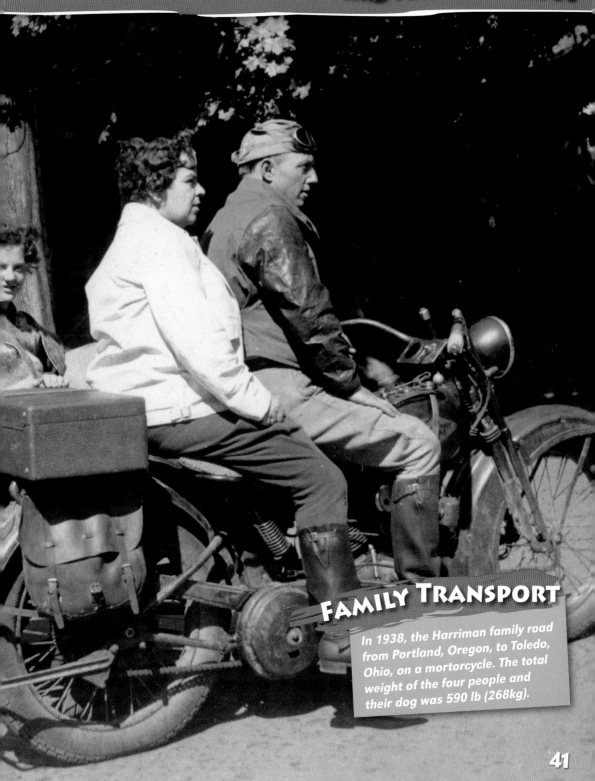

FAMILY TRANSPORT

In 1938, the Harriman family road from Portland, Oregon, to Toledo, Ohio, on a mortorcycle. The total weight of the four people and their dog was 590 lb (268kg).

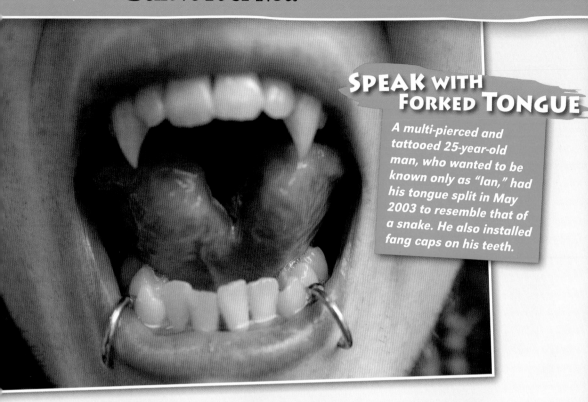

SPEAK WITH FORKED TONGUE

A multi-pierced and tattooed 25-year-old man, who wanted to be known only as "Ian," had his tongue split in May 2003 to resemble that of a snake. He also installed fang caps on his teeth.

FISH BONES

Chinese artist Liu Huirong recreates famous works of art in fish bones! She took two years and used more than 100,000 fish bones to complete a copy of "Spring's Back," a 300-year-old painting by Yuan Jiang. She has been making fish-bone pictures for more than 20 years. Every day she collects fish bones from roadside garbage bins and degreases, marinates, and chemically treats them before sticking them on to canvas.

BRANCHING OUT

For more than 25 years, performance artist David "The Bushman" Johnson has been alarming people on Fisherman's Wharf, San Francisco, by jumping out from behind branches as they pass by. He has been arrested over 1,000 times as a result of people not getting the joke.

BONE SCULPTURE

In 2001, U.S. artist Sarah Perry created "Beast of Burden," a 9-ft (2.7-m) rocketship made from horse and cattle bones! She has created other sculptures from hundreds of tiny rodent bones, which she has painstakingly extracted from owl pellets. She also makes art using junk that has been discarded in the Nevada Desert and once made a 700-lb (318-kg) gorilla from old rubber truck-tires.

RAW TALENT

Gabriela Rivera horrified visitors to an art gallery in Santiago, Chile, in 2005, by showing a video of herself with her face covered in raw meat. She said it showed the relationship people have with themselves each day when they look in the mirror.

WINTER WOOLLIES

In 2001, a group of volunteers in Tasmania, Australia, knitted turtleneck sweaters for a colony of rare Australian penguins to protect the birds against oil spills!

HAIR FORCE

Indian police have been trying to improve their public image by paying officers to grow mustaches. In 2004, chiefs in Madhya Pradesh announced a monthly mustache bonus of 30 rupees (about 50 cents) after research showed that officers with smart facial hair were taken more seriously. Mustaches are a sign of authority in India.

GHOSTLY PAYOUT

In 2001, an insurance company in Great Britain offered a "Spooksafe" policy for death, injury, or damage caused by a ghost or poltergeist.

TIME CAPSULE

At the 1957 Tulsarama Festival in Tulsa, Oklahoma, a brand new Chrysler car was buried in a time capsule, to be unearthed in 2007. People were asked to guess Tulsa's population in 2007. Whoever is closest wins the car; if that person is dead, the heirs get the car.

OVER YOUR HEAD

Shanghai, in China, saw the première of what was billed as the first acrobatic ballet—a combination of Western dance and ancient Chinese acrobatics. In this scene from "Swan Lake the Acrobatic," a ballerina balanced on her toes on the head of a male dancer.

IN A TWIST

Los Angeles contortionist Daniel Browning Smith, is otherwise known as The Rubberboy—he is so flexible he can cram his whole body into a box the size of a microwave oven.

IN DEPTH

When did you first discover your flexibility?
"I was four years old when I jumped off my bunk bed and landed in a perfect saddle split. I showed my father and he went to the library and brought me home pictures of contortionists—I tried to copy them, and I could. As a kid playing hide and seek I could hide in the sock drawer!"

How did you turn that into a career?
"When I was 18 the circus came through town where I grew up in Mississippi. I told my family I was joining it and would be back in three weeks—that was eight years ago."

What exactly can you do?
"I believe I am the most flexible person alive. Most contortionists can only bend one way—I can bend so far backwards the top of my head touches the seat of my pants, and so far forward I can kiss my own behind! I can also disconnect both arms, both legs, and turn my torso 180 degrees."

What is your favorite stunt?
"De-Escape—it is the complete opposite of Houdini's straitjacket routine. I have to dislocate my arms and squeeze into a locked straitjacket, then chain myself up with my mouth and flip myself into a box."

What else can you do?
"I can make my ribcage go up and my abdomen go down so you can see my heart beating through my skin! And I can get into a box about the size of a microwave. I get my shins in first, because I can't bend them, then my back, then my head and arms fill the holes. I have to slow down my breathing because my arms and legs put pressure on my lungs."

Does it hurt?
"I practice a stretch until just before it becomes painful, then hold it a bit until it feels normal, then stretch a bit further. The connective tissue between my bones is different genetically, inherited from both sides of my family. My father's father was in the military and it helped him to dislocate his hips when it was time to march. The stretches I do enhance that for me."

Have you ever got stuck?
"I can get through an unstrung tennis racquet or a toilet seat, but once a toilet seat got stuck around my torso with my thigh in the hole as well. I was home alone, and had to crawl into the kitchen and get a bottle of vegetable oil and pour it all over me. The seat finally came off—I just made a huge mess."

Are you working on future stunts?
"I'm trying to turn my head 180 degrees. I can get to about 175 degrees already. It's the only thing I've tried that's made me gasp—it's weird looking down and seeing your own butt!"

ROCK AROUND THE CLOCK

Thirty-six-year-old Suresh Joachim, from Mississauga, Ontario, spent 3 days 3 hours 3 minutes 3 seconds rocking in a rocking chair nonstop in August 2005. In the course of his challenge at the Hilton Garden Inn, Toronto, Ontario, he ate just one plain white bun, some noodle soup, three hard-boiled eggs, and one and a half potatoes. He also drank water and energy drinks, but not enough so that he would have to go to the toilet. His greatest fear was falling asleep, because of the need to rock continuously back and forth.

BLOOD STAINS

Mexican artist Teresa Margolles staged a 2005 exhibition in Metz, France, featuring clothing stained with human blood. She worked in a morgue for ten years and her display comprised clothes worn by corpses.

HAIR WEAR

Nina Sparre, of Vamhuf, Sweden, practices the art of Haarkulla, or "Hair Farming," creating art and clothing out of human hair!

LIVING BILLBOARD

Forty models lived in a 3-D billboard on the side of a building for two days in July 2005, creating New York City's first-ever live billboard. They were advertising a new fragrance from Calvin Klein. The models were told to create an illusion of a big party, 24 hours a day.

LAST RIDE OF YOUR LIFE!

Gordon Fitch took his passion for motorcycles to a new level when he started his Blackhawk Hearse business. For a fitting and dignified last ride, bikers can have their coffins drawn by a Harley Davidson motorbike.

CHOMPING CHAMP

Australian "Bushtucker Freddy" devours a locust during the 2005 Bug Eating Championships. He went on to win the competition that involved challengers from all over the world eating a variety of creepy crawlies, such as crickets, mealworms, hornets, and locusts.

CAR POLISH
You can't miss Yvonne Millner when she drives down the streets of Hopkins, South Carolina—hers is the car decorated in nail polish. She started by painting on a smiling face, but now she has designs and slogans all over her car, including a palm tree and the words "Hang Loose."

She spends three to four hours a day on the creation and has used more than 100 bottles of nail polish.

LONG MUSTACHE
Heads turn when Paul Miller, from Alta Loma, California, walks down the street. That's because his mustache is 10 ft (3 m) long! It takes him an hour to groom it each day.

47

Acknowledgments

FRONT COVER (t/l) Natasha Veruschka, (sp) Jim Mouth; 4 (l) Jim Mouth; 5 (l) Natasha Veruschka; 6–7 Leon Schadeberg/Rex Features; 7 Reuters/Chaiwat Subprasom; 8 Ben Philips/Barcroft Media; 9 Craig Barritt/Barcroft Media; 10 Malissa Kusiek/AP/PA Photos; 11 Mark Mirko/Rex Features; 12–13 Jim Mouth; 17 Indranil Mukherjee/AFP/Getty/Getty Images; 18 Reuters/Will Burgess; 20–21 Moses Lanham; 22 Reuters/John Gress; 23 Barcroft Media; 24 Reuters/Toby Melville; 25 Heather Insogna; 26 Natasha Veruschka; 28 Reuters/Alexander Demianchuk; 29 Reuters/Francois Lenoir; 30–31 Jim Mcnitt; 32 Photograph by Ma Qibing/Phototex/Camera Press; 33 Stuart Clarke/Rex Features; 34 Reuters/Kai Pfaffenbach; 36 Gary Roberts/Rex Features; 37 Chinafotopress/Camera Press; 38–39 Simon Burt/Rex Features; 42 Reuters/Chip East; 43 Reuters/Claro Cortes; 44–45 www.JulianCash.com; 46 Doug Hall/Rex Features; 47 Ben Philips/Barcroft Media;

KEY t = top, b = bottom, c = center, l = left, r = right, sp = single page, dp = double page

All other photos are from Ripley's Entertainment Inc.
Every attempt has been made to acknowledge correctly and contact copyright holders and we apologize in advance for any unintentional errors or omissions, which will be corrected in future editions.

Ripley's Believe It or Not!®

Believe It or Not!

WEIRD-ITIES!

Publisher Anne Marshall
Editorial Director Rebecca Miles
Assistant Editor Charlotte Howell
Text Geoff Tibballs
Proofreader Judy Barratt
Picture Researchers James Proud, Charlotte Howell
Art Director Sam South
Senior Designer Michelle Foster
Reprographics Juice Creative

Executive Vice President Norm Deska
Vice President, Archives and Exhibits Edward Meyer

PUBLISHER'S NOTE
While every effort has been made to verify the accuracy of the entries in this book, the Publishers cannot be held responsible for any errors contained in the work. They would be glad to receive any information from readers.

WARNING
Some of the stunts and activities in this book are undertaken by experts and should not be attempted by anyone without adequate training and supervision.

Published by Ripley Publishing 2013
Ripley Publishing, Suite 188, 7576 Kingspointe Parkway, Orlando, Florida 32819, USA

2 4 6 8 10 9 7 5 3 1

ISBN 978-1-60991-024-2

Some of this material first appeared in *Ripley's Believe It or Not! Expect... The Unexpected*

Library of Congress Cataloging-in-Publication data is available

Manufactured in China in February/2013 by Leo Paper
1st printing

Ripley's— Believe It or Not!®

WEIRD-ITIES!

BREAKING BOUNDARIES

Ripley PUBLISHING

a Jim Pattison Company

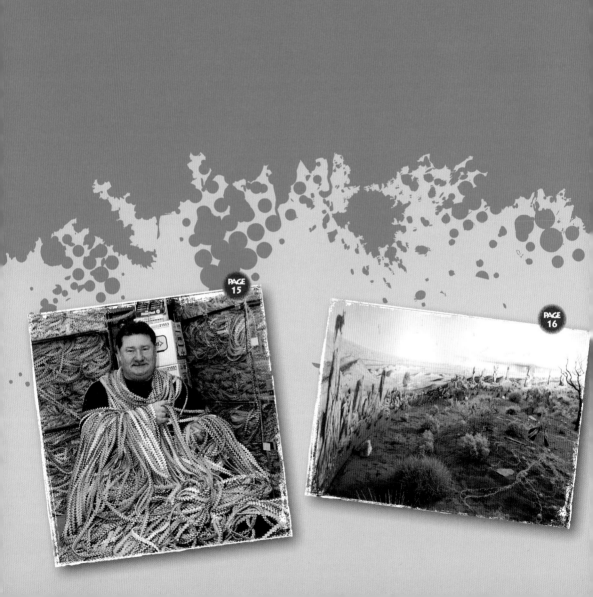

PAGE 15

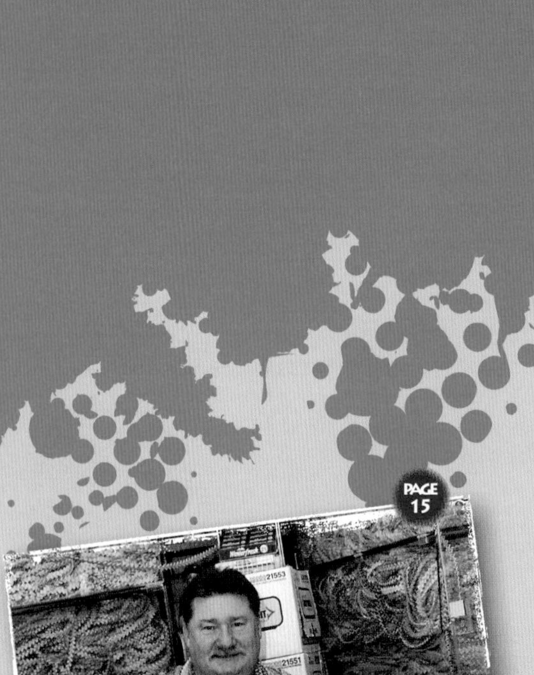

PAGE 16

BREAKING BOUNDARIES

On the edge. If you think you can push yourself to the limit you won't be so sure when you take a look inside. Read about the woman who wore a corset for over 20 years, the man who can eat 49 hot dogs in just 12 minutes, and the 9-mi (14-km) gum-wrapper chain.

PAGE 22

PAGE 38

BUILDING ACE

For the past 14 years, Bryan Berg has been creating some of the world's most famous buildings from playing cards. At the 2005 Canada National Exhibition in Toronto, the celebrated cardstacker amazed audiences with his detailed replicas of the Taj Mahal, the Colosseum, and the Pyramids.

Berg puts the finishing touches to a Gothic cathedral.

Thirty-seven-year-old Berg, who comes from Spirit Lake, Iowa, was introduced to cardstacking by his grandfather at the age of eight. By the time he was 17, Berg was building towers of cards over 14 ft (4.3 m) tall. In 1999, he built a 133-story tower that was 25 ft (7.6 m) high from 2,000 packs of cards. He needed scaffolding so that he could reach the very top. In February 2005, as part of the Asian tsunami relief effort, Berg worked for 18 hours a day, ten days straight, to construct a skyline of New York City. He used 178,000 playing cards, each of which represented a victim of the disaster. The Empire State Building, the Chrysler Building, and Yankee Stadium were all there in breathtaking accuracy.

Berg bases his card towers on carefully constructed grids. He says that the combined weight of the cards actually adds to the stability of the structure.

AIR GUITAR

At the 2005 Guilfest music festival in Guildford, England, 4,083 people gathered to play air guitars at the same time. With air-guitar "experts" on hand to dispense advice, the wannabee rockers mimed to "Sweet Child of Mine" by Guns 'n' Roses.

EGGS GALORE

At the annual Easter egg hunt at Rockford, Illinois, on March 26, 2005, an incredible 292,686 eggs were hunted for and found by 1,500 children in just 15 minutes. The event involved 200 volunteers, 156 bales of straw, and 1,000 hours of stuffing plastic eggs.

MODERN HOUDINI

Canadian escape artist Dean Gunnarson specializes in freeing himself from handcuffs and locked coffins. One of his most famous routines is the "Car Crusher," which he performed in Los Angeles, California, in 1990. First he was handcuffed and then chained into a 1970 Cadillac by the South Pasadena Chief of Police. Gunnarson's neck was chained to the steering wheel, his legs were bound to the brake pedal, and his arms were fastened to the doors. The Cadillac was then lifted into a car crusher, which was set in motion, its steel jaws closing menacingly. A mere

2 minutes 7 seconds later, Gunnarson amazingly leapt to freedom from his automobile prison, just a few seconds before the vehicle was completely destroyed by the merciless crusher.

PLANE SAILING

Canada's Ken Blackburn is no regular aviator—he deals strictly in paper airplanes. He has been making paper planes since the age of ten and broke his first record in 1983, when he managed to keep his creation airborne for 16.89 seconds. But he bettered that at the Georgia Dome, Atlanta, in 1998 with an unbelievable 27.6 seconds.

EGGSTRAORDINARY

Brian Spott, from Colorado, balanced 439 eggs on the floor at Melbourne's Australian Centre for Contemporary Art in 2005. He said the secret was to find the sweet spot on the base of an egg, adding: "You need a steady hand and a lot of patience."

8

PULLING TEETH

In June 1999, 36-year-old Krishna Gopal Shrivestava pulled a 270-ton boat a distance of 49 ft (15 m) in Calcutta harbor using only his teeth.

VOICE BROKE

Terry Coleman, of Denver, Colorado, sang continuously for 40 hours 17 minutes in July 2005. His target was 49 hours, but his voice gave out after 40. "The hardest thing was staying awake," he said afterward.

HARMONICA HARMONY

At Seattle's 2005 Northwest Folklife Festival, Andy Mackie led no fewer than 1,706 harmonica players in a rendition of "Twinkle, Twinkle Little Star" that lasted 13 minutes 22 seconds.

FISH SWALLOWER

In just one hour in July 2005, Indian yoga teacher G.P. Vijaya Kumar swallowed 509 small fish his mouth and blew them out of his nose! Kumar was inspired by American Kevin Cole, who blows spaghetti strands out of a nostril in a single blow. After successfully ejecting peas and corn through his nose in earlier exhibitions, Kumar turned to live fish.

WHEELCHAIR STAR

In July 2005, neuroscientist William Tan, from Singapore, covered 151 mi (243 km) in a wheelchair in just 24 hours by completing a staggering 607 laps of an athletics track. Two months earlier, the redoubtable Tan had completed 6½ marathons on seven continents over the course of only 70 days.

UNICYCLE FEATS

Between 1976 and 1978, Wally Watts, of Edmonton, Canada, rode a unicycle 12,000 mi (19,300 km) in various countries around the world. And through 1983 to 1984, Pierre Biondo, of Montreal, Canada, rode a unicycle around the entire perimeter of North America, just over 12,000 mi (19,300 km).

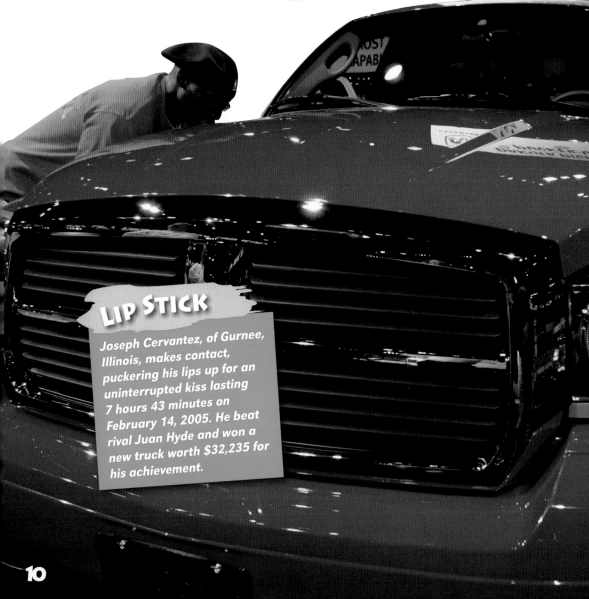

LIP STICK

Joseph Cervantez, of Gurnee, Illinois, makes contact, puckering his lips up for an uninterrupted kiss lasting 7 hours 43 minutes on February 14, 2005. He beat rival Juan Hyde and won a new truck worth $32,235 for his achievement.

BIRTHDAY BOWL

Seventy-year-old Jean Beal bowled 70 games in one day (one game for each year of her life), on June 29, 2005, to celebrate her birthday. It took her nearly 14 hours. Jean, from Hickory, North Carolina, said of the challenge: "I was just doing it to see if I could."

HULA HEROINE

Australian circus performer Kareena Oates created history in June 2005 by managing to spin 100 hula hoops around her waist for three full revolutions.

CHORUS LINE

In 2005, 15,785 workers in Tangshan City, China, all sang "Workers are Strong" simultaneously.

THE ONE THAT GOT AWAY

In May 2005, Tim Pruitt, of Alton, Illinois, caught a record 124-lb (56-kg) blue catfish in the Mississippi River. The monster-sized fish measured a staggering 58 in (147 cm) long and 44 in (112 cm) around. Alas, the fish, which was thought to be at least 30 years old, died the following week while being transported to a Kansas City aquarium where it was to go on public display.

NIGHT SKIING

Canadians Ralph Hildebrand and Dave Phillips water-skied for 56 hours 35 minutes around Rocky Point, British Columbia, in June 1994. They used spotlights and infrared binoculars during the night-time periods of the marathon.

ICE STATUE

Russian Karim Diab stood motionless in the freezing Moscow River for one whole hour. He had prepared for two years to accustom his body to surviving in the icy water for an hour without moving. He recovered with a hot bath, but was still too cold to talk.

BACKWARD BOWLER

Jim Cripps isn't content with bowling scores of more than 250—he does it backward! It all started as a joke. Jim, from Nashville, Tennessee, was clowning around at the lanes one afternoon when he suddenly made a decision to bowl backward. He turned his back on the pins, took a few steps, hurled the ball and got a strike! One of his friends bet him he couldn't bowl a 150 in reverse, but after six weeks of practice, Jim managed it.

Bowling backward, he rolled a 279 in a game that included 11 consecutive strikes.

BLIND DATE

In July 2005, Singapore's Nanyang Technological University staged a romantic event as part of its 50th anniversary celebrations, whereby 536 first-year undergraduates (268 couples) got together to stage a mass blind date.

LARGE DEPOSIT

In June 2005, Edmond Knowles walked up to a Coinstar machine at a bank in Flomaton, Alabama, and cashed in 1,308,459 pennies, which amounted to $13,084.59. He had started saving pennies in 1967, keeping the coins in a 5-gal (19-l) can. But, by the time of his huge deposit, he had collected so many that they were being stored in four large 55-gal (208-l) drums and three 20-gal (76-l) drums.

HOCKEY MARATHON

In June 2005, Canadian radio host Mike Nabuurs played air hockey for 48 hours straight, at a table in the lobby of McMaster University Medical Center, Hamilton, Ontario.

FASTEST FINGERS

Dean Gould, of Felixstowe, England, can lay claim to being amazingly dexterous. Over the past 20 years the

42-year-old father-of-three has shown that he has the fastest fingers and the handiest hands by setting new standards in such reaction-testing skills as beer-mat flipping, winkle picking, pancake tossing, coin snatching, and needle threading.

TONGUE-TIED

Using only his tongue, Florida firefighter Al Gliniecki tied 39 cherry stems into knots in three minutes in 1999. On another occasion, he tied an incredible 833 stems in one hour. Yet Al nearly wasn't around to put his talented tongue to use. While working as a lifeguard at Pensacola in 1982, he was struck by a bolt of lightning that threw him 38 ft (12 m) and blew the fillings out of his teeth.

BALLPARK MARATHON

In 2005, Mike Wenz and Jake Lindhorst saw 30 baseball games in 29 days—each in a different major-league ballpark. The 22-year-old buddies from Chicago began their ballpark marathon in New York's Shea Stadium on June 12 and finished at Miami's Dolphin Stadium on July 10.

HAPPY BIRTHDAY!

An incredible 27,413 birthday candles lit up New York City on August 27, 2005. Taking 1½ minutes, 50 people rapidly lit candles on top of a cake that measured 47 x 3 ft (14 x 0.9 m).

WRAP ARTIST

On March 11, 1965, a 14-year-old Canadian boy stuck a wad of Wrigley's gum in his mouth and carefully folded the wrappers into links. That night he scribbled an entry in his diary: "I started my gum-wrapper chain with 20 spearmint gum wrappers today."

Forty years later, Gary Duschl's gum-wrapper chain is made up of over one million wrappers and stretches for more than 47,000 ft (14,325 m) at his home in Virginia Beach, Virginia. To travel the length of the chain would take 9 minutes in a car moving at 60 mph (97 km/h)! What started out as a desire to have the longest chain in class, then in school, then in the area, has become a 630-lb (285-kg) monster. There is more than $50,000-worth of gum in Duschl's incredible chain.

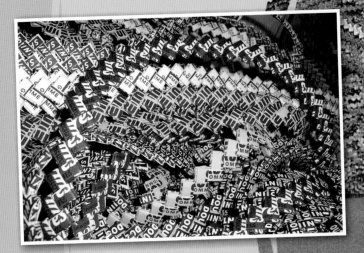

Many of the wrappers are sent in by well-wishers. Duschl admits that even he couldn't have chewed that amount of gum during the past four decades!

SKY HIGH

To celebrate her 99th birthday on February 17, 1996, Hildegarde Ferrera made a parachute jump over Hawaii. She came through the jump with nothing worse than a sore neck, but sadly died two weeks later from pneumonia.

HANDSTAND DISPLAY

A total of 1,072 people turned up at Indianapolis in 2005 to perform an astonishing display of simultaneous handstands. Participants in the challenge came from as far afield as Kansas, Texas, and Oregon.

GIANT SKIS

In February 2005, in Jacques Cartier Park in Ottawa, Ontario, 100 skiers traveled 330 ft (100 m) on a gigantic pair of skis, 330 ft (100 m) long.

CHECK MATES

An incredible 12,388 players turned out to take part in simultaneous chess matches at a public park in Pachuca, near Mexico City, one day in June 2005. Around 80 percent of the competitors were children.

LONG TRAIN

When Hege Lorence married Rolf Rotset in Norway in June 1996, her bridal train was 670 ft (204 m) long, and had to be carried by 186 bridesmaids and pageboys.

GET THE PICTURE

Australian artist Ando has created a huge painting of the outback, which measures an extraordinary 328 x 39 ft (100 x 12 m). Painted on a curved canvas, "The Big Picture" is complemented by more than 300 tons of red landscaped earth (see right), which adds to the image's 3-D effect. Only from certain angles are visitors able to see where 2-D meets 3-D.

ICY VOYAGE

After chasing a coyote on the ice near Canada's Prince Edward Island in 2001, foxhound Scooter was carried out to sea in a blizzard. She was rescued five days later after traveling 43 mi (70 km) on an ice floe across the Northumberland Strait.

SAUCY STORM

Most people would use a 14-oz (400-g) bottle of ketchup sparingly. Not Dustin Phillips from Los Angeles, California. In 1999, he drank 90 percent of a bottle through a straw in just 33 seconds (and wasn't sick)!

DELICIOUS WORMS

"Snake" Manohoran, a 23-year-old hotelier from Madras, India, ate 200 earthworms in 30 seconds in 2004. He said that he overcame any reservations about eating them by simply thinking of them as meat. He acquired the nickname from his trick of putting his pet snake up his nose and pulling it out through his mouth!

WHIP-CRACKER
Illinois entertainer Chris Camp cracked a 6 ft (1.8 m) bullwhip 222 times in one minute on the Mike Wilson Show in April 2005!

SHORT STORY

Adeel Ahmed, a 24-year-old Pakistani seen here being interviewed, is only 37 in (94 cm) high. He was born a normal child, but by the age of five had stopped growing.

CHILD PRODIGY
Michael Kearney did not sleep as much as other babies. Instead, he just wanted to talk. By the age of just five months, he was using four-word sentences, and at six months he calmly told a pediatrician: "I have a left-ear infection." He enrolled at Santa Rosa Junior College when he was just six years old and graduated two years later with an Associate of Science in Geology. In 1994, aged ten, he received a bachelor's degree in Anthropology from the University of South Alabama. He achieved a master's degree in Chemistry at 14 and was teaching in college at the tender age of 17.

HIGH FLYERS
A team from Edmonds Community College, Washington State, flew a kite continuously for more than 180 hours (7½ days) at nearby Long Beach in August 1982.

TWISTED WALK
Inspired by an item on the *Ripley's Believe It or Not!* TV show, an Indian teenager has perfected the art of walking with his heels twisted backward. Despite misgivings from his mother that he might injure his legs, Bitu Gandhi, from Rajkot in the state of Gujarat, practiced until he was able to walk 300 steps forward and 300 steps backward by twisting his ankles nearly 180 degrees.

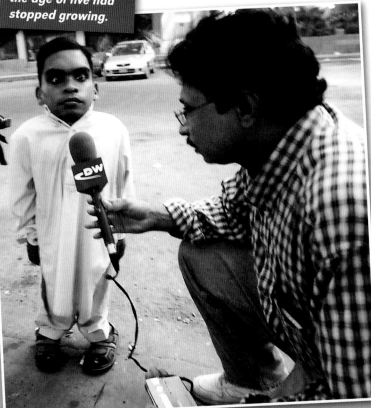

MORE THAN A MOUTHFUL

This appetite-busting hamburger, made by Denny's Beer Barrel Pub in Clearfield, Pennsylvania, on June 1, 2004, weighed about 11 lb (4.9 kg).

EAR WE GO

Lash Pataraya, 23, from Georgia, lifted 115 lb (52 kg) with his ears in Tbilisi in October 2003. He also used his ears to pull a minibus weighing 1½ tons a distance of 158 ft (48 m), by attaching it to his ears with string.

SWEET TREAT

Jim Hager, a dental-plan manager from Oakland, California, ate an astonishing 115 M&M's® with a pair of chopsticks in just 3 minutes in September 2003.

ENDURANCE TEST

Cathie Llewellyn, of Wintersville, Ohio, won a new car in 2005 after living in the vehicle for 20 days. She triumphed when her last remaining opponent gave up because she needed to use the bathroom. All contestants had been allowed a five-minute break every six hours during the challenge, which took place in a Steubenville, Ohio, shopping mall.

AERIAL WEDDING

Nobody in the world has done more skydives than Don Kellner. Don, from Hazleton, Pennsylvania, has more than 36,000 skydives to his name and his wife Darlene is no slouch either, having made around 13,000. Naturally

enough, their wedding in 1990 was conducted in mid-air, the ceremony being performed by fellow skydiver, the Rev. Dave Sangley.

FAST FINGERS

Barbara Blackburn, of Salem, Oregon, can type 150 words per minute for 50 minutes (37,500 key strokes), and has a top speed of 212 words per minute and an error frequency of just 0.002 per 100 words. Her secret is a special keyboard, which has vowels on one side and consonants on the other.

A KNIFE'S EDGE

TGT

Ripley's ~ **Believe It or Not!®**

22

The Great Throwdini is a world-champion knife-throwing minister from Freeport, New York, who takes the world of "impalement arts" to the extreme with his death-defying Maximum Risk act.

When and why did you become a knife thrower?
"My real name is the Rev. Dr. David Adamovich and for 18 years I was a professor of exercise physiology. When I was 50, I opened a pool hall and one of my customers brought in a small throwing knife. I threw it into a tree outside and struck it perfectly. Nine months later I came second in the world knife-throwing championship."

What is Maximum Risk?
"I'm one of the world's best in competition throwing, and I've converted that skill into a stage act called Maximum Risk. The name is a line from the French movie 'Girl on the Bridge,' about a knife thrower who persuades suicidal girls to be his assistants."

Do you just throw knives at your assistants?
"I throw knives, tomahawks, axes, and machetes—but I never throw 'at,' I throw 'around!' My assistant stands in front of a board, or is strapped on to the Wheel of Death while I throw two knives per revolution, one on each side of her. I also catch knives mid-air, and throw both right- and left-handed, blindfolded, and with my back to the board. I don't know why they call it 'impalement arts' because the last thing we want to do is impale our assistants. "

How fast can you throw?
"Throwing a single knife at a time, I can throw 75 in one minute. Throwing three knives at a time, my personal best is 144 knives around my partner in one minute."

Do you have any special techniques?
"I video what I do and watch it back—I study my hands very carefully. When I throw blind, I use sound to judge where to throw. My assistant sets me up facing the board, and I know exactly where she's standing."

Have you ever injured yourself or an assistant?
"I once had to stop because I stuck myself with the point of a knife and started bleeding from my fingers. Knives have bounced from the Wheel of Death and scraped the girl, but I've never impaled a girl."

Is it difficult to find willing assistants?
"Very! I don't just want a girl to stand there as my target— it's about the way she flirts with me and the audience, while facing danger."

Do you come from a performing family?
"Through my high school years I was a gymnast. I competed in the junior Olympics. One of my daughters is a surgeon who is very good with a knife in a different way! My wife Barbara was a knife thrower herself but retired—she has no wish to be my assistant."

JUST FOR LAUGHS

In 1992, American comedian Mike Heeman set out to tell as many jokes as possible in 24 hours. By the end of his marathon gag-fest, he had cracked no fewer than 12,682 jokes.

RIDING HIGH

In June 2004, Terry Goertzen, a pastor from Winnipeg, Canada, completed a 328-yd (300-m) ride on a bicycle constructed like a ladder that stood 18 ft 2½ in (5.5 m) high and was powered by a chain measuring 35 ft 8 in (11 m) in length.

MASS PILLOW FIGHT

No fewer than 766 people knocked the stuffing out of each other at Oregon State University in 2003 in a mammoth pillow fight. The event was organized by student Lige Armstrong as part of a class project.

MATH MARVEL

A 59-year-old man from Chiba, Japan, recited pi—or the ratio of the circumference of a circle to its diameter—to more than 80,000 decimal places during a 12-hour challenge in 2005. Akira Haraguchi started the attempt shortly after noon on July 1 and stopped at 83,431 decimal places early the following day. In doing so, he comfortably beat his previous best of 54,000 decimal places.

BALLOON BONANZA

In a bizarre challenge, students from Temasek Secondary School in Singapore set out to produce as many objects shaped from balloons as possible. In July 2005, a huge gathering of 1,471 students exercised their lungs to create 16,380 balloons in shapes that ranged from flowers to giraffes.

SELF-TAUGHT COWBOY

There aren't too many cowboys in Maryland, but Andy Rotz is an exception. The self-taught cowboy from Hagerstown—who learned his art from watching John Wayne and Clint Eastwood movies—can do more than 11,000 Texas skips, a maneuver that entails whipping a vertical loop of rope from side to side while jumping through the middle. He had to keep the rope spinning for 3 hours 10 minutes and perform a skip roughly every second.

SUPER BOWL

Suresh Joachim created bowling history in Toronto, Ontario, in June 2005, by bowling nonstop without sleep for 100 hours. To meet his challenge, he endured 360 games of bowling in which he achieved a fantastic 120 strikes. However, he also managed to break nine bowling balls!

IN PEAK CONDITION

On May 21, 2004, Pemba Dorjie Sherpa, a 27-year-old Nepali, climbed the upper reaches of the world's highest mountain, Mount Everest, in just 8 hours 10 minutes. Everest is 29,039 ft (8,851 m) high and Pemba's climb—from base camp at 17,380 ft (5,297 m) to the summit— usually takes experienced mountaineers up to four days.

WILD BILL'S BIKE

When William "Wild Bill" Gelbke decided to build a giant motorcycle at a Chicago workshop, he had no plans or blueprints. It took him eight long years, but when the Roadog finally appeared in 1965, it created quite a stir. The mammoth bike measured 17 ft (5.2 m) in length, weighed 3,280 lb (1,488 kg), had a frame built from aircraft tubing, and had a cruising speed of a cool 90 mph (145 km/h).

LAWNMOWER RIDE

As part of the Keep America Beautiful campaign, Brad Hauter, from Indiana, rode a lawnmower coast to coast across the U.S.A. He set off from San Francisco in April 2003 and arrived in New York 79 days later after a journey of more than 5,600 mi (9,012 km). The specially adapted mower had a top speed of 25 mph (40 km/h).

FULL HOUSE

Believe it or not, 15,756 players took part in a single game of bingo at the Canadian National Exhibition in August 1983.

BASKETBALL MARATHON

At New England's Beatrice High School gym between July 28 and July 30, 2005, players staged a 52-hour marathon basketball game. "Everyone was exhausted by the end of the game," said organizer Jim Weeks. Some players struggled through the early hours of the mornings and were ready to give up when they reached 40 hours, but they bravely battled on. The final score was 7,935 points to 6,963.

READING ALOUD

In March 2005, 1,544 students, from Pleasant Valley Middle School, Pocono, Pennsylvania, simultaneously read aloud *Oh the Places You'll Go* by Dr. Seuss.

HUMAN RAMP

Tim Cridland's feats are inspired by the mystics of the Far East. Through using "mind-over-matter" philosophy, he has taught his brain not to register the feeling of pain. He can swallow swords and dance on broken glass, but it is his car feat that he counts as his greatest achievement. While lying on a bed of nails with spikes 5 in (13 cm) long, he is able to endure the weight of a 1-ton car driving over him. His skin is not even punctured.

49-DAY FAST

Chen Jianmin, a doctor of Traditional Chinese Medicine, went 49 days without food in 2004, drinking only water.

An exponent of the practice of fasting, Chen entered the sealed glass cabin, measuring 160 sq ft (15 sq m), on March 20, 2004. The box was fixed 30 ft (9 m) high above the ground on a mountainside near Ya'an City. More than 10,000 visitors who turned out to watch the fast could see into Mr. Chen's house, except for two areas where he showered and used the toilet. While doing so he had to keep his head above a curtain to prove that he wasn't eating. Chen entered the box weighing 123 lb (56 kg) and emerged from the box at least 33 lb (15 kg) lighter. He claimed to have once gone 81 days without food.

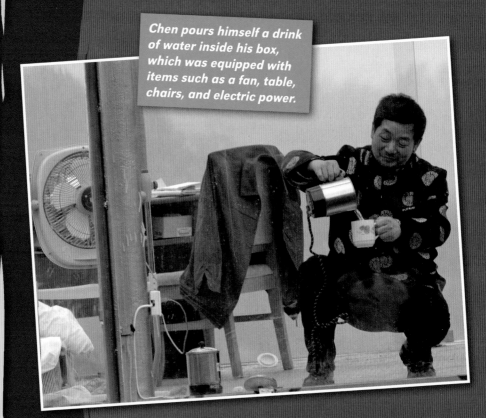

Chen pours himself a drink of water inside his box, which was equipped with items such as a fan, table, chairs, and electric power.

Chen takes a call. He claimed to have answered more than 8,000 telephone calls from all over China while in his box.

Suspended 30 ft (9 m) above the ground, Chen sits in his glass box watched over by his team below.

DING-DONG MERRILY

Canadian choir leader Joe Defries had music ringing in his ears after playing the handbells for nearly 28 hours straight. Joe, from Abbotsford, British Columbia, has been playing the handbells for more than 25 years and drew up a list of 1,300 tunes for his marathon solo venture in July 2005. Although he had never previously gone beyond 8 hours of solo ringing, Joe rose to the challenge, even finding time to crack jokes in the 30-second breaks he took after each tune.

HORROR CRAWL

Colorado Springs students Leo Chau and Sean Duffy crawled on their hands and knees for an agonizing 32 mi (51.5 km) through hailstorms and lightning in June 2005 to raise money for charity. The tortuous 44-hour crawl took its toll. Duffy suffered hallucinations and motion sickness while Chau was struck by severe dehydration.

ON A ROLL

In May 2005, to raise money for the Asian tsunami relief fund, students at the Cornell School of Hotel Administration, New York State, created a huge spring roll 1,315 ft (400 m) long. The monster hors d'oeuvre contained 3,500 spring-roll wrappers, 400 lb (180 kg) of vermicelli noodles, 250 lb (113 kg) each of carrots and cucumbers, and 80 lb (36 kg) of lettuce.

SUPER BOY

Eleven-year-old Bruce Khlebnikov tows an airplane with a rope attached to his hair on May 24, 2001, in Moscow, Russia. He has also pulled cars, lifted Russia's heaviest bodybuilder, torn thick books in half, and used his fists to break 15 ceramic plates that were attached together.

SPEED JUGGLING

Shawn McCue, from Sedalia, Missouri, was surfing the Internet when he came across a site for speed juggling. In high school he had been able to bounce a soccer ball on his foot as many as 600 times in three minutes, so he resolved to recreate past glories. In July 2005, in Jefferson City, he performed 155 juggles in 30 seconds, maintaining perfect balance throughout, while the ball never once rose more than 1 in (2.5 cm) off his foot.

BABY TALK

Born in 1982, Anthony McQuone, from Weybridge, England, could speak Latin and quote Shakespeare when he was just two years old.

YOUNG CAPTAIN

David Farragut, who later served as a naval officer during the American Civil War, was given command of his first ship when just 12 years old.

MUSICAL MINI

American singer Tori Amos began to play the piano at 2½ years of age and wrote her first song when she was just five years old.

FIRST EXHIBITION

Romanian painter Alexandra Nechita had her first solo exhibition in 1993 at the age of eight at a library in Los Angeles, California.

EYE-OPENER

Ever wanted a beer but couldn't find the opener? Bob Oldham, of South Carolina, was able to remove bottle tops with his eyes!

PRICKLY MATTRESS

This photograph of a young boy lying on a bed of nails was taken by missionary W.E. Morton in Benares, India, in 1926.

31

ELVIS LIVES!

They were all shook up in July 2005 in Cleveland, Ohio, when a total of 106 Elvis impersonators gathered on a high-school football field and performed a three-minute rendition of "Viva Las Vegas." Men, women, and children alike all donned gold shades and black plastic wigs for the occasion.

BUMPER BAGEL

For the 2004 New York State Fair, Bruegger's Bakeries created a bagel that weighed 868 lb (394 kg) and measured 6 ft (1.8 m) in diameter.

WHOLE LOTTA SHAKIN'

While campaigning in Albuquerque for election as New Mexico's governor in September 2002, Bill Richardson, a former U.S. Ambassador to the United Nations, shook 13,392 hands in 8 hours, smashing President Theodore Roosevelt's previously esteemed total of 8,513. At the end of the gruelling session, Richardson immediately sunk his hand into ice.

HIGH TEA

Dressed in formal evening wear, three explorers climbed into a hot-air balloon in June 2005 for an airborne dinner party. David Hempleman-Adams, Bear Grylls, and Alan Veal soared to a height of 24,262 ft (7,395 m) above Bath, England. Then, Grylls and Veal climbed 40 ft (12 m) down to a platform where, at a neatly laid dinner table, they ate asparagus spears followed by poached salmon and a terrine of summer fruits, all served in specially designed warm boxes to combat the freezing temperatures at altitude.

JUMPING FOR JOY

Gary Stewart, of Ohio, made 177,737 consecutive jumps on a pogo stick in 20 hours in May 1990.

TIGHTROPE CROSSING

Age was no bar to U.S. acrobat, balloonist, and tightrope–walker William Ivy Baldwin. During his lifetime, he made 87 tightrope crossings of the South Boulder Canyon, Colorado—the first when he was 14 and the last on July 31, 1948, his 82nd birthday! The wire was 320 ft (97.5 m) long and the drop was a very frightening 125 ft (38 m).

WAIST SPINNER

Ashrita Furman successfully hula hoops with a hoop that is 14 ft 7½ in (4.46 m) in diameter in New York's Flushing Meadow Park on July 15, 2005.

VICTORY TO RELISH

For the fifth straight year, it was a moment for Takeru Kobayashi to relish when he consumed 49 hot dogs in just 12 minutes!

In 2005, the 27-year-old speed eater, from Nagano, Japan, retained his crown at Nathan's Famous Fourth of July International Hot Dog Eating Contest at Coney Island, New York. Kobayashi, who stands 5 ft 7 in (1.7 m) tall and weighs just 144 lb (65 kg), beat runner-up Sonya Thomas, of Alexandria, Virginia, by 12 hot dogs, enabling the coveted Mustard Yellow Belt to return to Japan for the ninth year out of the past ten. Kobayashi's personal best is a staggering 53½ hot dogs in 12 minutes!

A brief moment before Takeru Kobayashi's success, he is seen struggling to keep his mouth closed as he valiantly attempts to chew and swallow his 49th hot dog.

DANNY'S WAY

Daredevil American skateboarder Danny Way created history in 2005 by clearing the Great Wall of China without motorized assistance. He hurtled down a 120-ft (36.5-m) specially constructed vertical ramp at a speed of approximately 50 mph (80 km/h) and leapt a 61-ft (19-m) gap to land safely on a ramp erected on the other side of the wall. The 31-year-old, from Encinitas, California, spent eight months planning the two-second jump.

NAILED DOWN

Lee Graber, of Tallmadge, Ohio, was sandwiched between two beds of nails with a weight of 1,659 lb (752.5 kg) pressing on top of him for 10 seconds in June 2000. The weight was lowered into position by a crane.

TREE PLANTER

Ken Chaplin planted 15,170 trees in a single day near Prince Albert, Saskatchewan, on June 30, 2001.

HIGHLY STRUNG

In June 2000, a team of 11 students from the Academy of Science and Technology at Woodlands, Texas, and their physics teacher, Scott Rippetoe, unveiled a fully playable Flying V guitar that measured 43 ft 7½ in (13.2 m) long and 16 ft 5½ in (5 m) wide. It weighed 2,244 lb (1,018 kg) and used strings that were 8 in (20 cm) thick and 25 ft (7.6 m) in length.

MIME MASTER

Bulgarian mime artist Alexander Iliev performed a 24-hour mime in July 2001 at the Golden Sands resort near Varna, Bulgaria, pausing for only a one-minute break every hour. His marathon effort featured more than 400 different pantomime pieces and saw him cover around 140 mi (225 km) on stage.

TOGA PARADE

In August 2003, in the town of Cottage Grove, Oregon, 2,166 people dressed in togas paraded down Main Street re-enacting the parade scene from the movie "National Lampoon's Animal House," which had been filmed in the town in 1977.

MAGGOT BATH

Christine Martin, of Horsham, England, sat in a bathtub of maggots for 1 hour 30 minutes in 2002.

LONG CUT

Jai Narain Bhati, a barber from Bhopal, India, cut the hair of 1,451 people over a 108-hour period in January 2002. His only breaks were for 10 minutes every hour.

HANDCYCLE TOUR

In 2005, paraplegic Andreas Dagelet set out from Coochiemudlo Island, Brisbane, to circumnavigate Australia on a handcycle— a sort of bicycle that is powered by arms and hands instead of legs and feet. The entire journey measured approximately 10,600 mi (17,000 km).

INSIDE JOB

In April 2005, a British couple drove the length of Europe without getting out of their car. Dr. James Shippen and Barbara May, from Bromsgrove, England, made the 2,000-mi (3,200-km) journey from John O'Groats, on the northern coast of Scotland, to the southern tip of Italy to demonstrate their invention, the Indipod, an in-car toilet.

MONSTER BOARD

In 1996, Todd Swank, from San Diego, California, built a skateboard for himself and his friends that was 10 ft (3 m) long, 4 ft (1.2 m) wide, and 3 ft (1 m) high. It weighed 500 lb (227 kg) and used tires from a sports car. He said he wanted to create a skateboard that no one would ever forget.

INFLATED LIZARD

If attacked, the chuckwalla, one of the largest lizards in the U.S., will crawl into a space between two rocks and puff itself up with air so that it can't be pulled out. It can inflate its lungs to increase its body size by as much as 50 percent.

HUMAN BELT

In September 1998, 1,000 students from the University of Guelph, in Ontario, Canada, formed an enormous human conveyor belt—passing a surfboard along the belt's entire length.

HEAVY LOADS

Pulling one fire truck may seem like a challenging feat, but not for this father and son who pulled two trucks at the same time!

Reverend Dr. Kevin Fast and his son Jacob Fast, 18, celebrated an unconventional Father's Day in June 2011 when they pulled two fire trucks at the same time that had a combined weight of approximately 160,000 lb (73,000 kg). Watched by hundreds of supporters, Kevin and his son, both from Canada, managed to pull the two trucks 98 ft (30 m) along the street in just 38 seconds. Strongman Kevin, who has already pulled a house and a plane by himself, put together the event to raise money for charity.

DOG TIRED

Andrew Larkey tried to walk 19 dogs simultaneously in Sydney, Australia, in May 2005. He began by being pulled in 19 directions before controlling 11 of the dogs single-handedly over the ⅔-mi (1-km) walk.

COFFIN ORDEAL

In May 2005 in Louisville, Kentucky, escapologist Aron Houdini (his legal name) spent an amazing 79 minutes inside a sealed coffin with no air. He was handcuffed, leg-cuffed, and chained inside the coffin. "I freaked out at first," admitted Houdini, who was able to communicate with his crew by way of a radio from inside the wooden box. "However, once I got my mind under control, I started what I had been practicing for almost a year. I slowed down my metabolism and then I concentrated on resting my entire body."

STONE SKIPPER

For years the leading exponent of the art of skipping a stone across the water was an American called Jerdone Coleman-McGhee. In 1994, he achieved 38 skips from a bridge on the Blanco River in Texas.

WURST IS BEST

In June 2005, 80 cooks from Leipzig, Germany, created a sausage that was 108 ft (33 m) long and required 294 broilers (grills) to cook it. The attempt to broil the sausage had to be called off when gusts of wind scattered the burning charcoal.

GROUP HUG

In April 2004, a staggering total of 5,117 students, staff, and friends from St. Matthew Catholic High School, Orleans, Ontario, joined forces—and arms!—to have an enormous group hug.

MOUNTAIN WRAPPED

Swiss authorities wrap some mountain glaciers with aluminum foil in the summertime to stop them from melting.

DOWNHILL CYCLE

Frenchman Christian Taillefer cycled down a glacier at 132 mph (212 km/h) in Vars, France, in 1998.

SNOW SPEED

When Mount St. Helens in Washington State, the highest peak in the U.S.A., erupted spectacularly in 1980, the avalanche on the north slope reached incredible speeds of 250 mph (400 km/h).

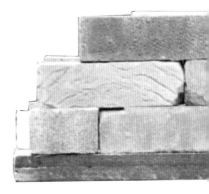

BRICK IT UP

Terry Cole balances 75 bricks weighing a staggering 328 lb (148.8 kg) on his head. Among other things, he has also carried a single brick held downward for 72 mi (116 km) and balanced 16 bricks on his chin!

HIGH DINING

Six Britons and one Australian took dining to new heights when they prepared and ate a five-course meal 22,000 ft (6,705 m) up a mountain in Tibet.

The diners dressed for the occasion with white ties and top hats and carried the tables, chairs, silver cutlery, floral centerpieces, candelabra, wine, and food all the way to the top.

ROCKETMAN

Texan Eric Scott took to the skies in England in April 2004, rocketing upward to 152 ft (46 m)—the height of a 12-story building. Eric remained airborne for 26 seconds. His "rocketbelt" was mounted on a fiberglass corset with two rocket nozzles and a belt that had basic controls for steering.

STRONG CHEST

In 1938, Rasmus Nielsen, a tattooed weightlifter from California, lifted 115 lb (52 kg) with his nipple.

INTERNET MARATHON

In November 1997, Canada's Daniel Messier spent 103 hours non stop surfing the Internet—that's more than four days!

GIANT NOODLE

Believe it or not, participants at Canada's Corso Italia Toronto Fiesta in 2003 created a spaghetti noodle that was an amazing 525 ft (160 m) long.

SORE HANDS

Peter Schoenfeld, of Ontario, Canada, chopped 209 wooden blocks by hand in just two minutes in October 2001.

MAKING WHOOPEE

In July 2005, following a baseball game in Bowie, Maryland, an incredible 4,439 Bowie Baysox fans sat on whoopee cushions simultaneously to create a gargantuan flatulence sound!

BIKER DUO

American couple Chris and Erin Ratay covered 101,322 mi (163,058 km) on separate motorcycles during a journey that took them through 50 countries on six different continents. They set off from Morocco in May 1999 and arrived home in New York in August 2003.

LENGTHY LECTURE

Errol Muzawazi, a 20-year-old lecturer from Zimbabwe, delivered a lecture lasting for 88 hours in 2005, talking non stop for more than three days. His audience at Jagellonian University in Krakow, Poland, fell asleep!

LUCKY LANDING

Czech climber Martin Tlusty survived a terrifying 1,000-ft (305-m) fall down the side of a mountain in Slovakia in 2005.

45

IN FLIGHT

Australian professional golfer Stuart Appleby drives off on one of the runways at Sydney Airport, Australia, on November 22, 2004. Appleby was competing against fellow golfers in a golf driving distance contest, which he won with a massive shot that reached an incredible distance of 2,069 ft 3 in (630.7 m)—more than one-third of a mile.

QUICK SOLUTION

If you need help with math, ask Gert Mittring. The 38-year-old needed just 11.8 seconds to calculate the 13th root of a 100-digit number in his head during a special challenge near Frankfurt, Germany, in 2004. He even solved the problem faster than onlookers with electric calculators.

SUNDAE BEST

On July 24, 1988, a giant ice-cream sundae was made by Palm Dairies, of Alberta, Canada. It featured an amazing 44,689 lb (20,270 kg) of ice cream, 9,688 lb 2 oz (4,394 kg) of syrup, and 537 lb 3 oz (244 kg) of delicious toppings!

BALANCING ACT

At the age of 12, Tim Johnston, of Piedmont, California, balanced 15 spoons on his face for 30 seconds in May 2004.

FREESTYLE RAP

Toronto rapper D.O. performed a freestyle rap that went on for 8 hours 45 minutes in July 2003.

HAVING A BALL

David Ogron has a ball every day of his life. In fact, in an average year he has 400,000 balls. The Californian hit on his unusual career some years ago when he was practicing with friends on the golf range. "We were seeing who could hit the ball the fastest. That's

CORSET CATHIE

Cathie Jung, now aged 73, has been wearing a corset, even when asleep, for more than 25 years. At 5 ft 6 in (1.68 m) tall and weighing 135 lb (61 kg), her waist measures a tiny 15 in (38 cm). The only time Cathie removes the corset is when she showers. Cathie's corset training started with a 26-in (66-cm) corset in 1983, when she had a 28-in (71-cm) waist. She gradually reduced the size of the corsets as they became comfortable.

when I realized I had a talent." With the help of ball-setter Scott "Speedy" McKinney, who puts each ball on the tee, Ogron hit 1,388 balls in 30 minutes in May 2005 at Louisville, Kentucky. And in July 2005, he hit 82 in one minute in Miami. On another occasion, he hit 10,392 balls in 24 hours.

CITY CHOIR

In what was an enormous gathering of Christmas carolers, 519 hardy souls braved the New York cold for a mass sing-along on the steps of Manhattan's General Post Office in December 2003.

Acknowledgments

FRONT COVER t/l) Laure A. Leber, (c) Ando Art, (b) Deborah Ann Duschl; 4 (l) Deborah Ann Duschl, (r) Ando Art; 5 (l) Laure A. Leber; 6–7 Norm Betts/Rex Features; 8 Reuters/Ho New; 9 Arko Datta/AFP/Getty Images; 10–11 Reuters/John Gress; 12 Sergei Karpukhin/Reuters; 13 Reuters/Ho New; 14–15 Deborah Ann Duschl; 16–17 Ando Art; 18 Aamir Qureshi/AFP/Getty Images; 19 Rex Features; 20 Ano Shlamov/AFP/Getty Images; 22 Laure A. Leber; 25 Reuters/JP Moczulski; 28 Sipa Press/Rex Features; 29 Reuters/China Photos; 30 East News via Getty Images; 33 Reuters/Shannon Stapleton; 34–35 Reuters/Seth Wenig; 36 (sp) Reuters/Jason Lee, (t) Reuters/China Daily Information Corp-CDIC; 41 Michael Fresco/Rex Features; 42–43 Photograph Camera Press; 44 Rex Features; 46 Reuters/Tim Wimborne; 47 Emily Baron/Barcroft Media

KEY t = top, b = bottom, c = center, l = left, r = right, sp = single page, dp = double page

All other photos are from the MKP Archives and Ripley's Entertainment Inc.
Every attempt has been made to acknowledge correctly and contact copyright holders and we apologize in advance for any unintentional errors or omissions, which will be corrected in future editions.

Ripley's Believe It or Not!®

WEIRD-ITIES!

Publisher Anne Marshall
Editorial Director Rebecca Miles
Assistant Editor Charlotte Howell
Text Geoff Tibballs
Proofreader Judy Barratt
Picture Researchers James Proud, Charlotte Howell
Art Director Sam South
Senior Designer Michelle Foster
Reprographics Juice Creative

Executive Vice President Norm Deska
Vice President, Archives and Exhibits Edward Meyer

PUBLISHER'S NOTE
While every effort has been made to verify the accuracy of the entries in this book, the Publishers cannot be held responsible for any errors contained in the work. They would be glad to receive any information from readers.

WARNING
Some of the stunts and activities in this book are undertaken by experts and should not be attempted by anyone without adequate training and supervision.

Published by Ripley Publishing 2013
Ripley Publishing, Suite 188, 7576 Kingspointe Parkway, Orlando, Florida 32819, USA

2 4 6 8 10 9 7 5 3 1

ISBN 978-1-60991-020-4

Some of this material first appeared in *Ripley's Believe It or Not! Expect... The Unexpected*

Library of Congress Cataloging-in-Publication data is available

Manufactured in China in February/2013 by Leo Paper
1st printing

Ripley's Believe It or Not!

WEIRD-ITIES!

SIMPLY UNBELIEVABLE

RIPLEY
PUBLISHING
a Jim Pattison Company

PAGE
6

PAGE
13

SIMPLY UNBELIEVABLE

Strange but true. Just when you thought
you had seen everything... Find out about
the Chinese man who uses his tongue
and fingers to paint, the man who set
himself up as a human dartboard, and
the astonishing two-headed peacock.

PAGE
17

PAGE
22

SOUNDS CRAZY

If Ken Butler's collection of musical instruments doesn't strike a chord with some listeners, it's hardly surprising. Ken dismisses conventional instruments in favor of the toothbrush violin, the golf-club sitar, or the hockey-stick cello.

New Yorker Ken created his first hybrid instrument in 1978 by adding a fingerboard, tailpiece, tuning pegs, and a bridge to a small hatchet, which he then played as a violin. The success of his ax violin led him to create more than 200 additional wacky instruments from such diverse objects as bicycle wheels, umbrellas, shotguns, and snow shovels. He usually chooses objects that are of roughly similar shape or proportion to the instrument that they then become.

The American musician and visual artist, who studied the viola as a child, has seen his creations displayed in museums and galleries in Peru, Europe, and Tokyo, as well as in several Ripley's museums. In 1997, he released an album—Voices of Anxious Objects—and he has performed with ensembles playing 15 of his instruments.

Musician Ken Butler, surrounded by some of his wacky instruments, including a hockey-stick cello in the top row.

To decide what would make a good instrument, Ken Butler seeks out objects that are relatively strong, but also relatively lightweight, and that allow for the placement of tuning pegs and strings.

STRONG BOY

When Rique Schill, from Jamestown, North Dakota, was pinned under the family Ford in 1984, his nine-year-old son Jeremy lifted the 4,000-lb (1,814-kg) car despite the fact that he weighed only 65 lb (30 kg) himself.

CAUGHT ON CAMERA

Michael Adams, from Manchester, England, chose an unwise target for a robbery—a shop specializing in security cameras. His raid was caught on eight different CCTV cameras!

CAR PLUNGE

In 2004, a car containing four teenage girls plunged over a 108-ft (33-m) cliff in Britain and flipped over three times before landing upright on rocks just a few feet from the swell of a raging sea. Incredibly, the girls' worst injury was a broken ankle.

STATIC SPARK

In 2002, Bob Clewis, 52, of San Antonio, Texas, survived a gas-station explosion after a simple spark of static electricity from his jacket ignited and engulfed him in flames.

ICE FALL

Although it was a warm summer's day, a cricket match near Faversham, England, was interrupted in 2005 when a huge chunk of ice fell from

LONG-LIFE BREAD

Vivien Anderson from Cambridgeshire, England, holds a bread roll that dates from World War I! It was given to her grandfather in a ration pack while he was serving in the conflict. Handed down through the family, the roll is estimated to be about 90 years old.

the sky and exploded onto the field. At the time, the sky was cloud-free and there were no aircraft in sight.

PERFECT PRESENT

Helen Swisshelm received the best Christmas present in 2001—a class ring that she had lost 53 years earlier! She last saw the gold-and-onyx ring in 1948 while swimming with friends in the Hudson River near her home in Cohoes, New York. She gave up hope of ever seeing it again until, more than half a century later, she received a call at her home in Lutz, Florida, from a nun at the Catholic school she had attended in Albany. A man with a metal detector scouring the Hudson had found a 1948 class ring bearing the school's shield and, via initials on the ring, the nuns matched the year and letters to Mrs. Swisshelm.

BULLET SURPRISE

After waking up with a headache, swollen lips, and powder burns in June 2005, Wendell Coleman, 47, of Jacksonville, Florida, went to hospital, where doctors found a bullet embedded in his tongue. Coleman didn't even know he'd been shot.

HOUSE SPARED

A houseowner in California must be the luckiest in the world. When the fires that devastated 663,000 acres (268,300 ha) of southern California in 2003 reached the wealthy suburb of Scripps Ranch, 16 mi (26 km) from San Diego, flames destroyed every house in the street except one.

SMOKING NEST

Fire chief Donald Konkle, of Harrisburg, Pennsylvania, decided that a house fire had been started when a bird picked up a smoldering cigarette while building its nest!

HIGH AND DRY

A seal was left high and dry when he found himself stranded on top of a post off the coast of Scotland. He had to wait nine hours before the tide came in sufficiently for him to roll back into the water.

TWO LAURAS

In June 2001, when Laura Buxton, from Staffordshire, England, released a balloon at her tenth birthday party, it traveled 140 mi (225 km) before being found in Wiltshire, England, by another ten-year-old girl, Laura Buxton! Not only did the girls share the same name and age, but they discovered they also had the same hair color and owned the same kinds of pet—a dog, a guinea pig, and a rabbit.

MISSING PEN

In 1953, Boone Aiken lost his engraved fountain pen in Florence, South Carolina. Three years later, while in New York City, Mrs. Aiken spotted a pen on the street next to their hotel. It was the lost one.

WALLET RECOVERED

When James Lubeck's wallet slipped from his pocket into Marblehead Harbor, Massachusetts, in 1966, he never expected to see it again. But in August 2005, he heard from Antonio Randazzo, who had hauled in the wallet's collection of credit cards in a netful of cod, flounder, and haddock 25 mi (40 km) away from where Lubeck had lost it.

SAME BIRTHDAY

Four generations of one family from Brisbane, Australia, share the same birthday—August 1. Norma Steindl was born on August 1, 1915; her son Leigh on August 1, 1945; Leigh's daughter Suzanna on, August 1, 1973; and Suzanna's son Emmanuel on August 1, 2003.

CHRISTMAS CHEER

When Matilda Close was born on Christmas Day 2003, in Victoria, Australia, believe it or not, she was the third generation of her family to be born on December 25! Her mother Angela and her grandmother, Jean Carr, were both born on Christmas Day.

HEART-STOPPER

While remodeling his bathroom in 2005, Nigel Kirk, from Burton-on-Trent, England, came within 0.04 in (1 mm) of dying after accidentally shooting himself in the heart with a nail gun. As he worked, 53-year-old Nigel slipped and managed to fire a 2-in (5-cm) steel tack straight into his heart. Luckily, the tack hit hard scar-tissue that had built up from an illness he had suffered 30 years earlier and just missed his vital heart vessels.

CHEWING CHALK

Rena Bronson, of Macon, Georgia, has a weird food craving—she eats chalk every day! She has been devouring chunks of the white clay called kaolin since 1992. Although it has made her constipated, she says that she likes the creamy consistency in her mouth.

DESERT ORDEAL

Max, a one-year-old golden retriever, survived after spending 3 weeks and 3 days stranded in the Arizona desert in 2005. Max ran off after his owner Mike Battles's truck was involved in a road accident. The dog was eventually found lying under a bush.

DOUBLE BIRTH

Twins Mary Maurer and Melanie Glavich gave birth to sons 35 minutes apart in 2005. They had the same due date, May 27, but both sisters went into labor early. They delivered in adjoining rooms at the same hospital in Middleburg Heights, Ohio.

LONG-LOST SOLDIERS

When Harry Dillon, sent out a letter addressed with nothing but a former comrade's name and a guessed city, the British ex-soldiers were reunited after 50 years!

LONG OVERDUE

A book was returned to a Californian library in 2005—78 years late! Jim Pavon said he discovered the copy of Rudyard Kipling's *Kim* in a box belonging to his late aunt, who had borrowed it from a library in Oakland in 1927. The library waived the fine of around $600 that had accrued on the overdue book.

HOLDING ON

Skydiver and sky-surfer, Greg Gasson regularly performs amazing stunts in the air. Here he hangs precariously over Eloy, Arizona, holding on by only one strap of his parachute, thousands of feet above the ground.

TYING THE KNOT

Boonthawee Seangwong and Kanjana Kaetkeow tied the knot on Valentine's Day (February 14) 2006, at Pattaya beach resort in Thailand.

The highlight of the Thai wedding, complete with chanting monks, centipedes, and scorpions, was that the "wedding room" took the shape of a coffin. The bride's 32 days spent in a plastic cage with 3,400 scorpions in 2002 can only be matched by the groom's 28 days in a cage with 1,000 centipedes in 2003.

INSECT INVASION

In November 2004, tourists holidaying in the Canary Islands, which lie off the northwest coast of Africa, received a shock when they were joined on the beach by a swarm of approximately 100 million pink locusts. Many of the migrating insects didn't live long enough to enjoy the scenery, however, having suffered broken legs and battered wings while crossing the sea in high winds and heavy rain.

UNWANTED GIFTS

Horst Lukas, of Iserlohn, Germany, was sent 12 bicycles, four boats, a mobile home, and dozens of tickets for rock concerts after a hacker spent $500,000 on eBay using his name.

FRUIT FIGHT

Every year, villagers at Ivrea in northern Italy re-enact a medieval battle by dressing up as soldiers and pelting each other with oranges!

BENDY BODIES

Contortionists with the State Circus of Mongolia perform extraordinary feats by bending their bodies into seemingly excrutiating shapes. Their limbs and joints are so flexible that they are able to bend into extreme positions.

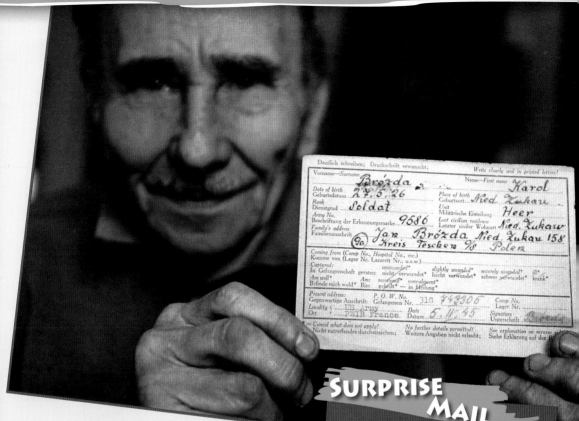

Former Polish soldier Karol Brozda, 79, now living in the Czech Republic, holds up a letter he sent to his parents from a U.S. prison camp in France in February 1945, assuring them that he was alive. His parents received the letter in March 2005!

CROC ATTACK

Shelly Hazlett has had 29 operations since being savaged by a huge crocodile during a show at her uncle's croc park in Australia. When Shelly slipped in mud, the reptile clamped its jaws on her lower torso and let go only when her father gouged out its eyes.

MAGNETIC POWER

Erika zur Stimberg is irresistible—to forks, spoons, and frying pans, which for the past 12 years have been flying toward her and sticking to her body. Doctors, in Brakel, Germany, are at a loss to explain her magnetism.

FALSE (TEETH) ALARM

Three years after losing his dentures in a fall, a Taiwanese man discovered in 2005 that they had been stuck in one of his bronchial tubes all the time. The 45-year-old sought medical attention when he started to have breathing difficulties. This lead to the amazing discovery of the missing dentures.

EXTRA FINGERS

Devender Harne, an 11-year-old boy from Nagpur, India, has a total of 25 fingers and toes. The five extra digits are functional and normal in size and do not prevent Devender playing his favorite sport of cricket.

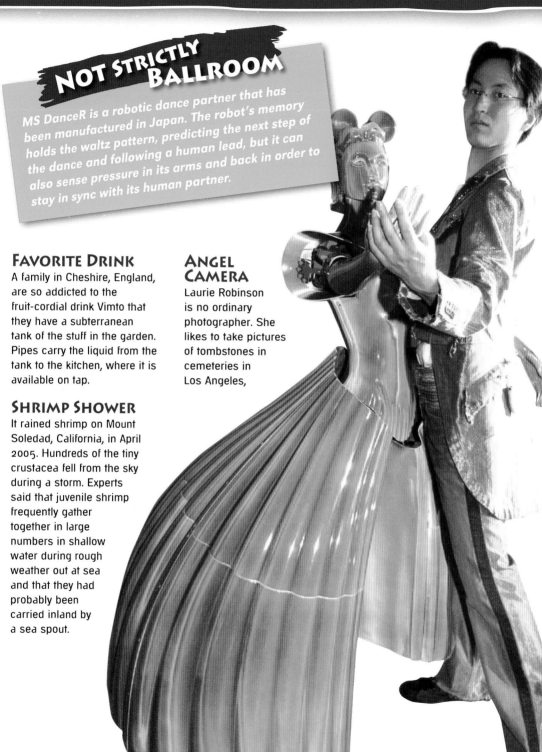

NOT STRICTLY BALLROOM

MS DanceR is a robotic dance partner that has been manufactured in Japan. The robot's memory holds the waltz pattern, predicting the next step of the dance and following a human lead, but it can also sense pressure in its arms and back in order to stay in sync with its human partner.

FAVORITE DRINK

A family in Cheshire, England, are so addicted to the fruit-cordial drink Vimto that they have a subterranean tank of the stuff in the garden. Pipes carry the liquid from the tank to the kitchen, where it is available on tap.

SHRIMP SHOWER

It rained shrimp on Mount Soledad, California, in April 2005. Hundreds of the tiny crustacea fell from the sky during a storm. Experts said that juvenile shrimp frequently gather together in large numbers in shallow water during rough weather out at sea and that they had probably been carried inland by a sea spout.

ANGEL CAMERA

Laurie Robinson is no ordinary photographer. She likes to take pictures of tombstones in cemeteries in Los Angeles,

ALL BUTTONED UP

Professor Leo Kongee could sew buttons to any part of his body, including his tongue, as seen here, as well as put skewers through his chest, cheeks, and ears. This photograph was taken in 1932.

California. And when she has her prints developed, ghosts and angels mysteriously appear in the photographs. She believes that the spirits show up in her pictures because of the positive energy she sends out.

LION GUARD

Believe it or not, a 12-year-old Ethiopian girl owes her safety to a pack of lions. The girl was abducted in June 2005 by seven men who wanted to force her into marriage, but the kidnappers were chased away by three lions that amazingly then stood guard over the girl for at least half a day. A police sergeant said: "They stood guard until we found her and then they just left her like a gift and went back into the forest. Everyone thinks this is some kind of miracle." A wildlife expert suggested that the girl's crying might have been mistaken for the mewing sound of a cub, which would explain why the lions didn't eat her.

SHOCKING EXPERIENCE

A man built up at least 30,000 volts of static electricity in his jacket simply by walking around the Australian city of Warrnambool, Victoria, in September 2005. Frank Clewer left a trail of scorch marks, carpet burns, and molten plastic behind him.

CRUSHING BLOW

Two men escaped from a Kentucky jail in 2005 and hid in a garbage truck—only for their bodies to be discovered in a nearby landfill the following day. The jailbirds hadn't realized that, to prevent exactly this kind of escape, the prison requires that all garbage be compacted twice before it leaves the grounds.

NAILED IT

Experiencing toothache and blurry vision, Patrick Lawler, of Denver, Colorado, went to a dentist in January 2005, only to learn that he had shot a 4-in (10-cm) nail through his mouth into his skull with a nail gun!

HEADLESS FOWL

On September 10, 1945, farmer Lloyd Olsen chopped off 5½-month-old Mike's head with an ax in readiness for the cooking pot, but the headless rooster continued pecking for food around the farm at Fruita, Colorado!

Olsen visited Los Angeles, San Diego, Atlantic City, and New York working the sideshows with his "Wonder Chicken" Mike.

Olsen decided to spare Mike and began feeding him grain and water with an eyedropper. Although most of Mike's head was in a jar, part of his brain stem and one ear remained on his body. As the majority of a chicken's reflex actions are controlled by the brain stem, Mike was able to function relatively normally.

Over the next 18 months, the chicken's weight increased from 2½ lb (1.1 kg) to 8 lb (3.6 kg) and, insured for $10,000, Mike toured the U.S.A. as the "Wonder Chicken," with Lloyd charging 25 cents for a peek. Finally, he choked on his way back from an appearance in Arizona. Olsen was unable to find the eyedropper used to clear Mike's open esophagus and Mike died.

Mike the Headless Chicken would "peck" for food and "preen" his feathers, just like the other chickens on the farm.

GHOST RADAR

This pocket-sized gadget aims to help people avoid "other-world" spirits. Shown here being used in a Tokyo cemetery, it claims to detect "unknown energies, ghosts, and spirits," by sensing tiny variations in magnetic turbulence, light, and temperature, and then giving position and movement. Instructions contain details on eight types of specter that range from harmless lost souls stuck in this world to evil spirits.

HAPPY ACCIDENT

Eddie May Jr., of Georgia, choked on a piece of food while driving, blacked out, then hit a passing car. The impact knocked the food from his throat and he awoke uninjured!

POT SHOT

While sitting on the toilet in April 2005, an off-duty Texan police officer accidentally shot a man. Officer Craig Clancy was answering a call of nature in San Antonio when his gun fell from its holster as he pulled down his pants. In trying to catch the gun, he grabbed the trigger and fired two bullets, one of which went through the cubicle wall and grazed the leg of a man who was washing his hands at the time.

INCRIMINATING EVIDENCE

After ordering a pizza and asking for a job application form, a man suddenly produced a gun and robbed a Las Vegas pizza parlor of $200 in June 2005. But police didn't have to do much detective work to catch him. He left behind the partially completed form, which included his name and address.

DOZED OFF

A cargo plane circled for more than half an hour in March 2005 because an air-traffic controller at Nice Airport, France, had fallen asleep.

OLD NEIGHBOR

Gilbert Fogg, of Nettleham, England, discovered that his neighbor Tom Parker was actually a long-lost comrade from World War II, whom he thought had died in battle!

BAIL BLUNDER

After being arrested for possession of counterfeit money in 2005, fraudster Darrell Jenkins, from Springfield, Massachusetts, tried to pay his $500 bail using fake notes!

DOG'S DINNER

A man from Schaarbeek, Belgium, set his apartment on fire in April 2005 after trying to cremate his pet dog on a barbecue and using far too much gasoline!

TEA THIEF

A man who stole a tractor-trailer truck in Washington State in 2005 had to call 911 for medical help after drinking from a cup he found in the cab. What he thought was a refreshing drink was in fact the truck driver's tobacco spit!

KING OF CUBES

Believe it or not, 14-year-old Shotaro Makisumi, from Japan, can solve a "3 x 3 x 3" Rubik's cube puzzle in a mere 13.72 seconds.

THE GREAT ESCAPE

The Dark Master of Escape, Canadian Steve Santini, also known as "The World's Most Extreme Escape Artist," puts the fear back into escapology with his blend of heavy metal and medieval torture.

How did you become interested in escapology?

"I did a book report for school on Houdini, and then started to experiment on my own. There were no instruction books—my parents kept getting calls: 'Your kid's jumping into our pool wrapped in bike chains."

How did it develop?

"I broke out of my first jail cell at a police station when I was 14 (I was put in there voluntarily!). I used to buy up old cuffs and locks, rip them apart, and see how they worked. I didn't know trick locks existed—I just learned how to defeat normal mechanisms."

Have you ever feared for your life during a stunt?

"On New Year's Eve 2005, when I performed the Cremation Chamber. It was watched by an audience of 35,000 people and 15 million live on television—the most ever to witness a single escape. I was in a vault with walls just one-eighth of an inch thick, and I was handcuffed and padlocked to a chain welded inside the door. On three sides of the vault were propane flame throwers—I was supposed to be out within one minute, when the temperature hit 400°F and the air became unbreathable. But one of the cuffs jammed, and I had to hold my breath until I could break free."

What other escapes have you performed?

"Lots—my favorites include escaping from a nailed and padlocked coffin submerged under 30 ft of water, and breaking out of a maximum security cell on Canada's Death Row, which had held the last man to be publicly hanged in that country."

What makes your shows different?

"I got tired of the image of escapologists in glitzy suits in Vegas. I wanted to remove the magic from it—by doing all escapes in full view of the audience. What really grabs people has to involve pain and danger. I use sinister heavy-metal music to play that up."

Why "Dark Master"?

"I came up with that not because I'm Satanic or because I'm portraying an evil person, but because I'm facing devices from people's nightmares, from the darkest periods of human history. I combine modern technology—like being pulled toward a chain saw—with ancient devices, like thumb screws and iron maidens."

Do you use hypnotism or contortionist techniques?

"I'm not a contortionist—I'm not a svelte guy! I use hypnotism techniques to focus. But it basically comes down to extreme stubbornness and an incredibly high pain tolerance."

Do you get nervous beforehand?

"Terribly. Every time I do these things, there's genuinely the chance that something will go horribly wrong. Once you're in, you can't panic though—if you do, you're done."

Are you working on any future projects?

"I want to be stretched on a medieval rack and have that lowered under water. No-one's ever got off a rack, let alone a submerged one. No, I'm not a masochist—I just know what will make people go 'whoa!'."

POTATO RING

Forty years after losing her wedding ring in a potato field, a German farmer's wife found it again while eating—it was inside a potato!

BLACK SPOT

In 1966, Christina Cort narrowly escaped death when a truck smashed into her home in Salvador, Brazil. She was still in the same house 23 years later when another truck crashed through the wall—driven by the same man.

IN THE STARS

Born in 1835, the year of Halley's comet, U.S. writer Mark Twain said that as he had come into the world with the comet, so he would pass with it. The comet returned in 1910 and Twain died that April, aged 74.

NIGHT CAP

Russian Vladimir Rasimov drank so much vodka that he fell asleep between train tracks and didn't wake up even when a 140-ton cargo train passed over him.

LOST DRIVER

In 2002, a train driver delayed hundreds of passengers for more than an hour, near Birmingham, England, after admitting he didn't know the route.

PERILOUS PUTT

Harold Parris, who has been playing golf regularly for 55 years, made the mistake of teeing off without his glasses in April 2005. Parris managed to land the ball on the back of an alligator while playing a round at the Robber's Row golf course, South Carolina!

SCREEN DAMAGE

When four horses broke out of their field in Hausen, Germany, in April 2003, only three survived. One horse was killed instantly when he raced across the road and was hit by a car, crashing through the windscreen. Miraculously, the 26-year-old driver was unhurt.

25

SHINING EXAMPLE

The average light bulb lasts no longer than 1,000 hours. But a carbon filament bulb has been burning in the fire department at Livermore, California, for more than 100 years!

Since being installed in 1901, the four-watt bulb has burned through the birth of powered human flight, women being granted the vote, two world wars, space exploration, 19 U.S. presidents, and 25 Olympic Games. Visitors come from as far away as South Africa and Sweden to check out the famous bulb. Engineers attribute its longevity to a combination of low wattage and filament thickness.

Such is the worldwide interest in the Livermore light bulb that it has its own official website, complete with a live webcam that allows browsers to see that it is still burning.

What makes its survival all-the-more remarkable is that before a local reporter uncovered its history in 1972, Livermore firefighters often batted it for good luck as they clung to the side of the departing fire truck. It has also experienced countless near misses from footballs and Frisbees. Now it is treated like a precious stone. As Tim Simpkins, Inspector with the Livermore-Pleasanton Fire Department, says: "I don't want to be on duty when and if it ever goes out."

Appropriately, the town slogan—adopted in the 1920s because of the area's clean air—is "Live Longer in Livermore."

Wright Brothers Flight 1903	Ford Makes Model-T 1908	Television Invented 1927	Nuclear Age Begins 1945	Pres. Kennedy Assassinated 1963	Pres. Nixon Resigns 1974	PC's Sold By IBM 1981	Internet Growth 1993
Flagpole Raised 1906	WW I 1914	Women Get The Vote 1920	WW II 1941	Disneyland Opens 1955	Man Lands On The Moon 1969	Titanic Found 1985	Berlin Wall Falls 1989
Light Bulb Installed 1901	Livermore 1st Rodeo 1918	Stock Market Crashes 1929	Lawrence Livermore Lab 1952	Woodstock & Altamont 1969	Lightbulb Moved 1976	LPFD Formed 1996	Lightbulb Century 2001
1901	1920	1940	1960	1980			2001

As the world's oldest-known working light bulb, when the Livermore Fire Department bulb was moved to its new home in 1976, it was handled with the greatest care. The bulb was granted Code 3 status and transported with truck lights flashing and sirens wailing.

ANIMAL ARTIST

Koopa the turtle, owned by U.S. artist Kira Varszegi, has sold more than 100 pieces of his own artwork. He creates the paintings by covering his underbelly in paint and sliding around on a canvas. The works usually sell for around $135 a piece.

POETIC JUSTICE

After two U.S. thieves stole a checkbook from the home of Mr. and Mrs. David Conner, they went to a bank with a $200 check made out to themselves. The female teller asked them to wait a minute, then called security. The teller was Mrs. David Conner.

HEAVY BREATHING

Three police cars raced to answer an emergency at a house in Lake Parsippany, New Jersey, one night in August 2005, only to be told by the owner that she had been teaching her German shepherd dog to make 911 calls. The 911 operator heard only "heavy breathing."

SHOT BY DOG

Bulgarian hunter Vasil Plovdiv was shot by his own dog in 2005 when he tried to knock a bird out of its mouth with the butt of his rifle. The German pointer refused to drop the quail and instead leaped at Plovdiv, knocking the trigger and peppering his chest with shot.

BRIGHT SPARK

After locking himself out of his still-running car in Glen Burnie, Maryland, in 2005, an 82-year-old man had the idea of stopping the engine by removing all the gasoline. Unfortunately, he used an electric vacuum cleaner to siphon the fuel and, when a spark ignited the vapors, he was taken to hospital with burns.

TIGHT SQUEEZE

Contortionist Hugo Zamoratte— "The Bottle Man"—dislocates nearly every bone in his body and can squeeze into a bottle!

SMITH PARTY

In Vermont, all 57 of the David Smiths listed in the state's phone books got together for a "David Smith Night!"

DRAWBRIDGE DRAMA

A 79-year-old grandmother had an incredible escape in 2005 after she was left dangling 100 ft (30 m) in the air from a drawbridge. Retired teacher Helen Koton was crossing a canal in Hallandale Beach, Florida, when the drawbridge began to rise. She clung on to the railing as the bridge rose to its full height, leaving her hanging in the air, her handbag swinging from her ankle. Drivers alerted the bridge operator, who lowered Helen back to the ground.

THIN MATERIAL

Physicists from Manchester, England, and Chernogolovka, Russia, have managed to create a flat fabric called "Graphene," which is only a single atom thick!

CHURCH AFLOAT

In 2003, the 2,000-sq-ft (185-sq-m) Malagawatch United Church was moved by water and road 20 mi (32 km) to its new home in Highland Village, Iona, Nova Scotia.

HIDDEN BULLET

For 25 years, Adrian Milton, of New York, had a bullet in his skull but didn't know it. He remembered an incident back in 1976 when blood had suddenly spurted from his head, but he always assumed that he'd been hit by debris from a building site. In fact he'd been shot in the head. His secret emerged in 2001 during a routine visit to the doctor.

CASH FLOW

Two motorcyclists lost $20,000 in cash in 2005 when their backpack burst open on a highway near Winchester, England. Although drivers stopped to help, strong winds blew the notes across the road and only a small portion of the money was recovered.

WHAT'S IN A NAME?

Even by the standards of Martha Stewart's colorful career, the U.S. kitchen goddess came up with a moment to remember in September 2005. On her TV show, she gathered no fewer than 164 Martha Stewart namesakes. They included Martha Stewarts who were married to men with equally famous names—a Jimmy and a Rod—and even a bulldog named Martha Stewart.

HEAD SPACE

Karolyne Smith, of Salt Lake City, Utah, offered her forehead for sale on eBay as the site for

BACKWARD HULA

At the age of just ten, Joyce Hart, of New Jersey, could do a backward somersault through two hoops.

a permanent, tattooed advertisement. The winning bid of $10,000 was made by the Golden Palace online casino.

BODY TALK

Believe it or not, an Indian man lived with his mother's corpse for 21 years. Syed Abdul Ghafoor kept the embalmed body of his mother in a glass casket at his home in Siddavata and even consulted the preserved corpse before making important decisions.

FUTURE VISION

One of the most popular crazes in Las Vegas is the "morph booth," where as many as 300 couples a day line up to see what their virtual reality child would look like. The fotomorphosis machine merges you and your partner's images to produce a supposedly accurate simulation of any future offspring. Some couples are reportedly using the machine before deciding whether or not to get married!

TOAD TOXIN

Dogs in Australia's Northern Territory are getting high by licking toxins from the backs of cane toads. Local veterinarian Megan Pickering said that some dogs were becoming addicted to the hallucinogens and she had treated more than 30 that had overdosed on bufo toxin.

TWO-HEADED PEACOCK

This two-headed peacock was raised on a farm in Texas, and lived to be almost two years old. It was taxidermied by Tim Dobbs, of Midland, Texas, in 2003. Ripley has yet to perform DNA testing to determine if the two heads do indeed belong to the same bird.

PICKLED DRAGON

Scientists at Britain's Natural History Museum could hardly believe their eyes in 2003 when confronted with a pale baby dragon, preserved in a jar of formaldehyde.

The dragon had apparently been discovered by David Hart, the grandson of a former museum porter, during a garage clear-out in Oxfordshire.

Accompanying the find were documents suggesting that the dragon had originally been offered to the Natural History Museum in the late 19th century by German scientists, but that the museum had rejected it as a hoax.

While modern scientists began to re-examine the tale, it emerged that the 19th-century museum curators were right—the dragon was a hoax. But, the current story was also a hoax! Hart had invented it in order to promote a novel written by Allistair Mitchell. The dragon had been made for a BBC TV series *Walking With Dinosaurs*.

The dragon was actually built by BBC model makers and turned out to be part of an elaborate publishing hoax.

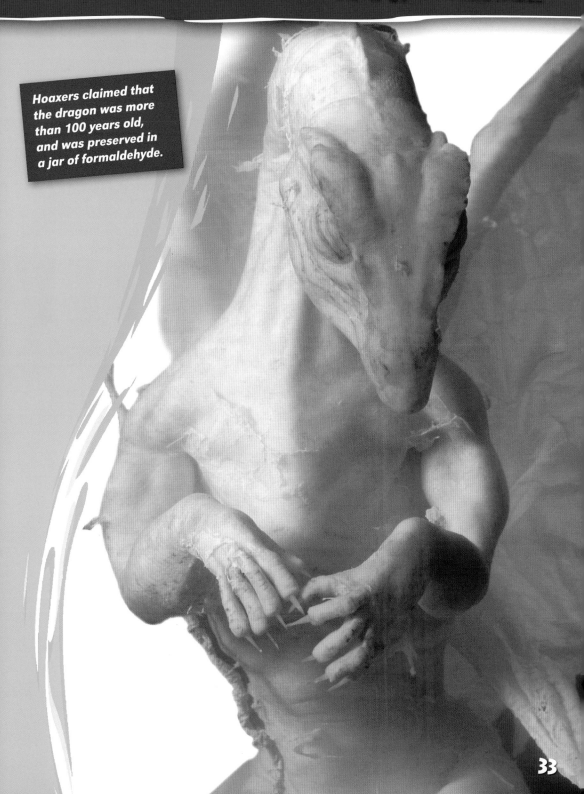

Hoaxers claimed that the dragon was more than 100 years old, and was preserved in a jar of formaldehyde.

TWIN TRAGEDIES

In March 2002, Finnish twin brothers, aged 71, were killed in identical bicycle accidents along the same road, two hours apart. Both men were hit by trucks, the second twin's fatality occurring half a mile from the first's.

YAK-SKIING

Yak-skiing is the new extreme sport that is catching on in Manali, India. A person on skis stands at the foot of a hill holding a bucket of nuts while attached by a long rope fed around a pulley to a yak at the top of the hill. When the bucket is rattled loudly, the yak charges down the hill, yanking the skier up the slope.

IRONIC THEFT

Among items stolen from All Souls Church in Peterborough, England, in July 2005, was a 2-ft (0.6-m) high statue of St. Anthony of Padua, who is the patron saint of lost and stolen items.

DESPERATELY SEEKING...

The Lutheran Church of Landeryd, Sweden, put a "wanted" advertisement in a local newspaper asking for churchgoers.

KNITTED ART

The Canadian artist Janet Morton's Domestic Interior, a piece that includes this knitted telephone and table, is just one of her hand-knitted wool creations. In another work, entitled Cozy, she covered a cottage situated on Toronto Island in more than 800 recycled sweaters!

PLAYING WITH FOOD

The Vienna Vegetable Orchestra is seen here performing in London, England, at a concert that included only vegetables! Formed in 1998, the orchestra consists of musicians playing instruments made almost exclusively of vegetables.

NAME CHECK

On business in Louisville, Kentucky, in the late 1950s, George D. Bryson registered at room 307 at the Brown Hotel. When he jokingly asked if there was any mail for him, the clerk gave him a letter addressed to the previous occupant of the room, another George D. Bryson!

TOTALLY BARKING

Mark Plumb, aged 20, of Houma, Louisiana, was arrested in August 2005 after he allegedly ran barking from a house and bit the local mailman on the shoulder.

SNIFF AND TELL

A German telecommunications company is presently developing the world's first cellular phone that will alert users when their breath is bad!

LUCKY CALL

When stranded in the Andes, Leonard Diaz from Colombia was rescued after a phone company employee called him on his expired cell phone to ask if he wanted to buy more time!

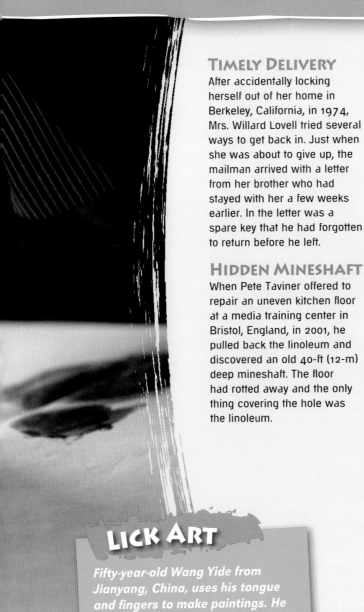

TIMELY DELIVERY

After accidentally locking herself out of her home in Berkeley, California, in 1974, Mrs. Willard Lovell tried several ways to get back in. Just when she was about to give up, the mailman arrived with a letter from her brother who had stayed with her a few weeks earlier. In the letter was a spare key that he had forgotten to return before he left.

HIDDEN MINESHAFT

When Pete Taviner offered to repair an uneven kitchen floor at a media training center in Bristol, England, in 2001, he pulled back the linoleum and discovered an old 40-ft (12-m) deep mineshaft. The floor had rotted away and the only thing covering the hole was the linoleum.

LICK ART

Fifty-year-old Wang Yide from Jianyang, China, uses his tongue and fingers to make paintings. He is one of the few artists still making traditional Chinese paintings using this method.

REGISTERED HAIR-DO

The "comb-over," in which a partially bald person grows hair long on one side and then combs it over the bald spot, is a U.S. patented invention!

PHOTO FIT

Awiey Hernandez was arrested in 2005 when he went to the 90th Precinct station house in Brooklyn, New York, to check on the status of a friend and inadvertently stood directly in front of his own "Wanted" poster!

PIG SAVIOR

Joanne Altsman owes her life to Lulu, her Vietnamese pot-bellied pig. When Joanne suffered a heart attack while on a trailer home holiday on Presque Isle, Pennsylvania, in 1998, Lulu squeezed out of the trailer's dog flap, pushed open the gate and waddled out into the middle of the road where she lay on her back with all four trotters in the air to stop the first passing car. Sure enough, a driver stopped, followed Lulu back into the trailer and found Mrs. Altsman semi-conscious. Doctors later said Joanne would have died within 15 minutes but for the pig's actions. Lulu received a bravery award and a big jam doughnut.

SHOCK FACTOR

The Great Voltini, Welsh electrocution artiste Sebastian Vittorini, loves nothing more than sending half a million volts of electricity through his body until lightning shoots from his fingers.

IN DEPTH

How did you become interested in electricity?
"I saw a cabaret act with an electric chair and I was fascinated to know how it worked, so I started building one myself. It went from there!"

What is your most famous act?
"The 'Lightning Man' act. I stand or sit on top of a huge Tesla coil—a 14ft-high column of wire named after its inventor Nikola Tesla and made by manufacturer HVFX. It transforms electricity into about half a million high-frequency volts—my body basically becomes a human conductor, and sparks and lightning strands shoot out through my fingertips."

Does it hurt?
"Actually, when you do it right, it's a pleasant kind of tingly feeling. It's only when you do it wrong that it hurts."

What are the dangers involved?
"When you get it wrong, your muscles contract involuntarily, which is very unpleasant—it's the same effect as when a person who has got an electric shock is thrown across the room. It can also cause cardiac arrest—people have died doing this kind of act. Long-term, it can cause partial paralysis owing to long-term nerve damage."

Why do you take the risk?
"So far, I've been shocked only a few times and had minor burns from the sparks. The most frightening thing is that when I'm on the machine, I can't control it myself—so my safety is in someone else's hands. But when I'm doing it, it's amazing. The lightning strands are constantly waving about in front of me. It's the most beautiful thing I've ever seen—I absolutely love it."

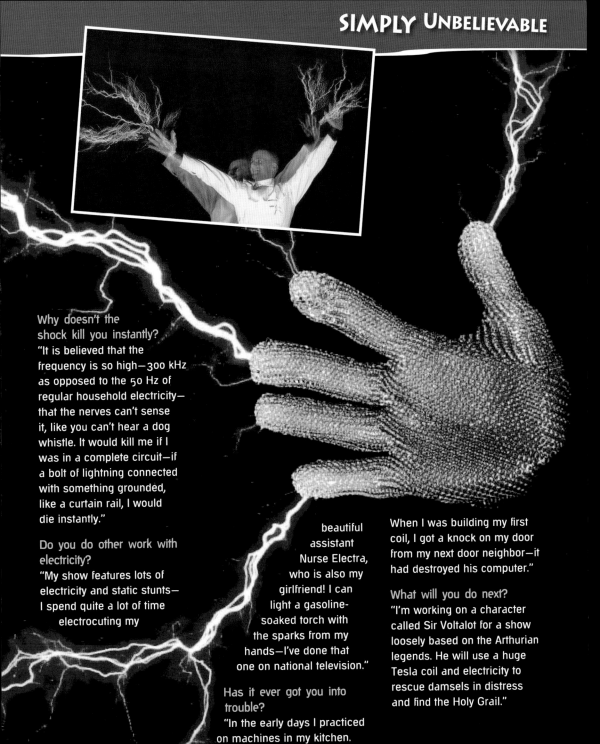

Why doesn't the shock kill you instantly?
"It is believed that the frequency is so high—300 kHz as opposed to the 50 Hz of regular household electricity—that the nerves can't sense it, like you can't hear a dog whistle. It would kill me if I was in a complete circuit—if a bolt of lightning connected with something grounded, like a curtain rail, I would die instantly."

Do you do other work with electricity?
"My show features lots of electricity and static stunts—I spend quite a lot of time electrocuting my beautiful assistant Nurse Electra, who is also my girlfriend! I can light a gasoline-soaked torch with the sparks from my hands—I've done that one on national television."

Has it ever got you into trouble?
"In the early days I practiced on machines in my kitchen.

When I was building my first coil, I got a knock on my door from my next door neighbor—it had destroyed his computer."

What will you do next?
"I'm working on a character called Sir Voltalot for a show loosely based on the Arthurian legends. He will use a huge Tesla coil and electricity to rescue damsels in distress and find the Holy Grail."

AMAZING MEDITATION

In December 2005, Ram Bahadur Bomjon, aged 15, from southern Nepal, claimed to have mastered the art of meditation to such an extent that he had gone without food and water for more than seven months. He plans to meditate for six years to achieve Enlightenment.

2005, he was horrified to find that there were no clovers to be found anywhere in the grounds. Kaminski feared that his great rival, Edward Martin Sr., a retiree of Soldotna, Alaska, would seize the opportunity to expand his own collection of 76,000 four-leaf clovers.

SLICE OF FORTUNE

A slice of singer Justin Timberlake's half-eaten French toast (complete with fork and syrup) sold on eBay for a staggering $4,000.

BANK FOLLY

Thomas E. Mason was charged with robbing a Winona, Minnesota, bank in June 2005, having been arrested nearby and identified by bank staff. The main evidence against him was his hold-up note, which began: "Hi, I'm Thomas Mason."

UNLUCKY CLOVER

Despite spending more than half his life in U.S. jails, George Kaminski has collected nearly 73,000 four-leaf clovers. He found all of them in the grounds of various Pennsylvania prisons, but when he was moved to a minimum-security facility in

MAD LEAP

A man was injured in 2005 when he jumped from a car traveling at 60 mph (96 km/h) in an effort to retrieve a cigarette that had blown out of the passenger-side window. Jeff Foran suffered trauma to his eyes, nose, and chin.

PARK PATROL

In an incredible feat of endurance, Christopher Calfee, a 38-year-old schoolteacher from Richmond, Virginia, ran around a park for nearly 92 hours in September 2005 without stopping for sleep. For four days and four nights he lapped Chesterfield's Pocahontas State Park. Apart from a three-hour halt to recover from the effects of dehydration, Calfee's only other breaks were for food at the end of each 25-mi (40-km) stint. But he never slept during the 316-mi (508-km) run. The pain was so intense that he had to protect his blistered toes with duct tape.

NIGHTTIME MOWER

Ian Armstrong, from Cheshire, England, got up to mow the lawn in the middle of the night while sleepwalking.

DRIVING BLIND

Stephen Hearn, from Birmingham, England, crashed his car at 70 mph (113 km/h) while sleepwalking near his home. When Stephen was found, he was in his pajamas and still snoring.

CORN LADY

In 1938, Virginia Winn, of Texas, stitched 60,000 grains of corn onto an evening dress, one by one. The gown weighed 40 lb (18 kg).

DOG TRAIN RIDE

When Archie the black labrador became separated from his owner at a Scottish railway station in 2005, he decided to take the train, not only choosing the right one, but also getting off at the correct station! When the Aberdeen to Inverness train pulled in to the station, Archie, having lost sight of his owner and perhaps fearing a long walk home, trotted aboard. The clever dog got off 12 minutes later at the next stop, Insch, his local station.

DELAYED REVENGE

In 1893, Texan Henry Ziegland jilted his girlfriend, as a result of which she killed herself. Bent on revenge, her brother shot Ziegland in the face, but the bullet only grazed him before lodging in a nearby tree. A full 20 years later, Ziegland was using dynamite to uproot that same tree when the explosion blasted the bullet from the trunk. The bullet struck Ziegland in the head, killing him.

BERMUDA TRIANGLE

While riding a moped in Bermuda in 1975, a man was killed by a taxi. A year later, his brother was killed riding the same moped after being hit by the same taxi, driven by the same driver. The taxi was even carrying the same passenger.

ELVIS RELICS

Among the many Elvis Presley relics that have sold on eBay are a branch from a tree ($900) and a hanging plastic fern ($750), both from his Graceland home, and a ball from his pool table ($1,800). However, a tooth said to be from Elvis's mouth failed to sell when no one bid the asking price of $100,000.

WAVE RIDER

Brazilian surfer Serginho Laus achieved a lifetime's ambition in June 2005 when he rode one continuous wave for 33 minutes, and a distance of 6.3 mi (10.1 km). He was able to ride the wave up the mouth of the Araguari River in northeast Brazil thanks to a "bore" created by a change in the tides.

UNDERWATER MAIL

The island nation of Vanuatu in the Pacific Ocean has opened the world's first underwater post office, which is manned by postal workers in diving gear!

SUPER SELLER

Bargain hunter Suzie Eads, of Rantoul, Kansas, has sold so many items on eBay that she has been able to build a house for her family with the proceeds. She has auctioned more than 17,000 items altogether, including a discarded beer can for $380. She even drives with the licence plate EBAY QUN.

CLIP CHAIN

Eisenhower Junior High School, in Taylorsville, Utah, is a school with a difference. The pupils have a habit of setting themselves amazing challenges. On March 26–27, 2004, the students created a "Mega Chain" that measured 22.17 mi (35.68 km) long and used 1,560,377 paper clips. They took 24 hours and divided the team into different roles to achieve this incredible feat.

MIND-BENDER

Magician Paul Carpenter, from Houston, Texas, performs the art of psycho-kinetics, or metal bending, wowing audiences across the U.S.

LIGHTNING CONDUCTOR

With Carl Mize, lightning doesn't just strike twice—it's struck four times already! In 2005, Mize was hit for the fourth time, while working on the University of Oklahoma campus. Mize was hospitalized for four days before being discharged.

BULLETPROOF CASE

British manufacturers have devised a special bulletproof briefcase. If the user is fired at, the brown leather case can be flipped open and used as a shield able to withstand handguns up to a .44 Magnum.

PUMPKIN PADDLERS

Howard Dill grows pumpkins partly for their seeds and partly for carving out for racing. He cultivates an oversized variety of pumpkin called Atlantic Giant, and after selling the seeds he donates the hollowed-out fruit for use in the famous annual pumpkin paddling regatta at Windsor, Nova Scotia, Canada. In the 2005 event, 40 competitors paddled their way across Lake Pesaquid while sitting in pumpkins that weighed more than 600 lb (272 kg). The winner usually

In 1934, a fallen redwood tree, which was about 2,000 years old, was converted into an auto highway in the Giant Forest, California.

manages to get round the course in about 10 minutes.

UNINVITED GUEST

When Beverly Mitchell returned to her home in Douglasville, Georgia, after a two-week holiday, she discovered that the lights were on and a strange car was parked in her driveway. Another woman, a stranger, had moved in, redecorated the rooms, and was even wearing Mitchell's own clothes.

FLYING NUN

Madonna Buder has definitely got the triathlon habit. As well as being a Canadian record-holder and Ironman legend, she leads a quieter life as a Roman Catholic nun. Now in her seventies, Sister Madonna, from Spokane, Washington, has completed well over 300 triathlons. She took up running in 1978. Before entering her first Boston marathon, she sought permission from the local Bishop to take part.

LIFTED CAR

Despite fracturing her spine and damaging two vertebrae in a car crash near Washington, England, Kyla Smith managed to lift the one-ton car—about 20 times her own weight—6 in (15 cm) off the ground in the attempt to free her trapped friend.

STING FOR YOUR SUPPER

A Chinese man not only catches wasps, he also eats them! Zhong Zhisheng, from Shaoguan City, does not charge people for removing wasps nests from their homes, on condition that he is allowed to take the insects home and fry them.

45

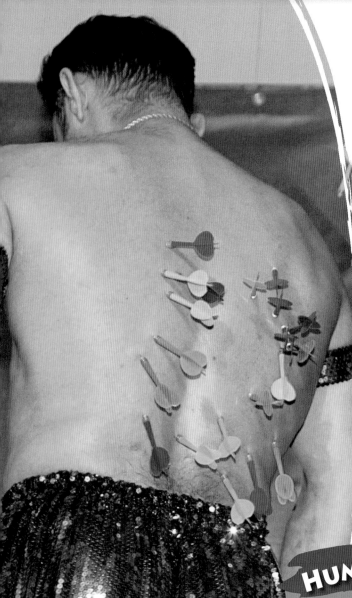

PACKED CHURCH

Canadian bride Christa Rasanayagam didn't exactly want her wedding in Ontario in 2004 to be a quiet affair. She was accompanied up the aisle by no fewer than 79 bridesmaids, aged from one to 79, who jostled for room with the groom's 47 best men.

BUMPY LANDING

A German driver who was using an airport runway to practice high-speed driving had a lucky escape in 2005 when a plane landed on his roof! The 55-year-old Porsche driver was traveling at more than 100 mph (160 km/h) near Bitburg when the bizarre collision occurred.

SHORT TERM

Believe it or not, there was a man who was president of the U.S. for just one day! When James K. Polk's term ended at noon on Sunday, March 4, 1849, and his successor, Zachary Taylor, refused to be sworn in until the following

HUMAN DART

Evgeny Kuznetsov, from Dzerzhinsk, Russia, set himself up as a human dartboard in Moscow in January 2006. Darts were hurled at his back— amazingly, without drawing a drop of blood.

YOUNG AT HEART

Although she is an impressive 96 years old, Peggy Barrett regularly takes to the skies in a glider. She and other 90-and-over pensioners from Gloucester, England, have formed the Gliding Nonagenarians.

day, David Rice Atchison, the president pro tem of the Senate, technically ruled the country in the intervening period. Asked what he did on that historic day, Rice admitted that he mostly slept after a succession of late nights.

NIAGARA PLUNGE

In October 2003, Kirk Jones, of Canton, Michigan, went over Niagara Falls without safety equipment and lived. Tourists saw Jones float by on his back in the swift Niagara River, plunge over the 180-ft (55-m) Horseshoe Falls on the Canadian side, then drag himself out of the water onto the rocks below.

PARACHUTE AHEAD

Parachutist Maria Ganelli, aged 40, had a fortunate escape in August 2005 when she landed in the middle of Italy's busy Adriatica Highway. She had planned to come down in a nearby field, but gusting winds pushed her off her chosen course and stunned drivers were forced to swerve to avoid hitting her.

Acknowledgments

FRONT COVER (b/l) Jerilyn Tabor, Alison Slon, Doug Levere, (t/r) Scott Stewart; 4 (l) Jerilyn Tabor, Alison Slon, Doug Levere; 5 (r) Scott Stewart; 6–7 Jerilyn Tabor, Alison Slon, Doug Levere; 8 Chris Radburn/PA Archive/PA Photos; 9 Dougie Hendry/Rex Features; 11 Joe Jennings; 12–13 Reuters/Sukree Sukplang; 14 Reuters/China Daily Information Corp-CDIC; 15 Drahoslav Ramik/CTK/Camera Press; 16 Reuters/Ho New; 18–19 Troy Waters; 20 Sutton-Hibbert/Rex Features; 21 Noah Berger/AP/PA Photos; 22 Scott Stewart; 23 Ken "Spear" Flick and Steve Santini; 24–25 Andy Reed/Barcroft Media; 25 (t) DPA Deutsche Press-Agentur/DPA/PA Photos; 26 Steve Bunn; 27 Dick Jones; 28 Jessica Hill/AP/Press Association Images; 29 CP Canadian Press/Canada Press/PA Photos; 32–33 Reuters/Allistair Mitchell; 34 Ben Philips/Barcroft Media; 35 Reuters/David Bebber; 36 Feature China/Barcroft Media; 38–39 www.voltini.com; 40 Reuters/Gopal Chitrakar; 43 R. Clayton Brough and Eisenhower JHS; 44 Paul Carpenter; 46 Reuters; 47 Barry Batchelor/PA Archive/PA Photos

KEY t = top, b = bottom, c = center, l = left, r = right, sp = single page, dp = double page

All other photos are from Ripley's Entertainment Inc.
Every attempt has been made to acknowledge correctly and contact copyright holders and we apologize in advance for any unintentional errors or omissions, which will be corrected in future editions.

Ripley's Believe It or Not!

WEIRD-ITIES!

Publisher Anne Marshall
Editorial Director Rebecca Miles
Assistant Editor Charlotte Howell
Text Geoff Tibballs
Proofreader Judy Barratt
Picture Researchers James Proud, Charlotte Howell
Art Director Sam South
Senior Designer Michelle Foster
Reprographics Juice Creative

Executive Vice President Norm Deska
Vice President, Archives and Exhibits Edward Meyer

PUBLISHER'S NOTE
While every effort has been made to verify the accuracy of the entries in this book, the Publishers cannot be held responsible for any errors contained in the work. They would be glad to receive any information from readers.

WARNING
Some of the stunts and activities in this book are undertaken by experts and should not be attempted by anyone without adequate training and supervision.

Published by Ripley Publishing 2013
Ripley Publishing, Suite 188, 7576 Kingspointe Parkway, Orlando, Florida 32819, USA

2 4 6 8 10 9 7 5 3 1

ISBN 978-1-60991-023-5

Some of this material first appeared in *Ripley's Believe It or Not! Expect... The Unexpected*

Library of Congress Cataloging-in-Publication data is available

Manufactured in China in February/2013 by Leo Paper
1st printing

Ripley's Believe It or Not!

WEIRD-ITIES!

AMAZING ANIMALS

Ripley PUBLISHING

a Jim Pattison Company

PAGE
9

PAGE
28

AMAZING ANIMALS

Curious critters. If you think people are astounding, you haven't met these incredible creatures! Discover the potty pig Olympics, the tiny 50-cm (20-in) horse, and the ugliest dog you have ever seen!

PAGE 33

PAGE 34

WEB OF INTRIGUE

Instead of using traditional canvases, Enrique Ramos, of Mexico City, known as "The Fly Guy," creates tiny portraits of famous people on flies, feathers, beans, animal bones, and even bats!

Marlon Brando painted on a quails egg, measuring only 1 in (2.5 cm) high.

Without the help of any kind of magnification, Ramos has handpainted Da Vinci's "*Mona Lisa*" on a bird feather, a bean, and a stuffed bat. Often his pictures take under two minutes. He has even painted seven faces on a single human hair!

Sometimes Ramos uses no paint at all. He made a portrait of The Beatles from more than 60 dung beetles and hundreds of butterfly wings, and a bust of Abraham Lincoln from the hair of his son and daughter.

Ramos likes to paint subjects on real cobwebs too. He is unable to correct mistakes and also considers himself lucky if one-third of the gathered webs survive to form one of his cobweb paintings.

This bat was created to celebrate Halloween and the Mexican Day of the Dead festival and depicts Freddy Krueger from Nightmare on Elm Street, Lon Chaney as the Wolfman, and Bela Lugosi as Dracula.

A depiction of Spiderman—one of Ramos's most recent works—is made from nearly 20 lb (9 kg) of large wolf spiderwebs, and stands more than 2 ft (60 cm) in height.

These butterflies are part of a 35-piece Mexican history series. The first shows the Spanish conquistador, Hernando Cortez, and the second depicts the tragic Aztec-Mayan love story of Popoca and Miztla.

DUCK DIALECTS

It sounds quackers, but an English scientist has discovered that ducks have regional accents. Ducks in London are noisier than those in rural Cornwall as they have to raise their voices to compete with traffic.

THE YAP OF LUXURY

Dudley's bakery, in Fort Myers, Florida, is a dog's dream come true. Created by Vickie Emmanuele, the bakery offers specially made fancy gourmet treats and dog cakes.

GOLF-BALL GUZZLER

Doctors in England removed 28 golf balls from the stomach of a German shepherd who frequently takes walks along a golf course with his owner.

VANISHING ACT

Seven years after mysteriously disappearing, Ewok, a nine-year-old Shih Tzu, suddenly returned to Crofton, British Columbia, home of Jim and Barbara Reed in 2001.

BARKING MATH

Alissa Nelson, of Urbandale, Iowa, has a mongrel named Oscar who can do math addition problems. He answers a variety of mathematical sums by barking. For example, when asked the sum of two and two, he responds with four barks.

INHERITANCE KITTY

In the 1960s, San Diego doctor William Grier left his entire fortune of $415,000 to his two 15-year-old cats, Brownie and Hellcat.

SURVIVED FALL

Andy, a cat owned by Florida senator Ken Myer, fell 16 floors (200 ft/61 m) from a building in the 1970s—and survived!

DOG'S HOME

As a reward for the dog saving her from a 2001 house fire, actress Drew Barrymore placed her $3-million Beverly Hills home in trust with her golden labrador Flossie so that it would always have a roof over its head.

FEELING SLUGISH

These sea slugs certainly stand out from the crowd. They are called nudibranchs, and they get their venom and stings from the food they eat, which includes poisonous corals, sea sponges, and sea anemones. Nudibranchs wear bright colors to advertise their toxic skin to predators.

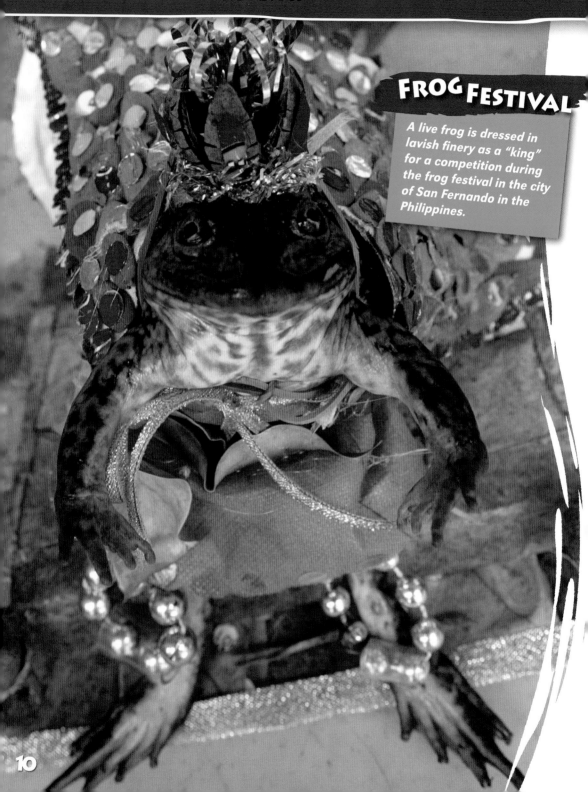

FROG FESTIVAL

A live frog is dressed in lavish finery as a "king" for a competition during the frog festival in the city of San Fernando in the Philippines.

CANINE CANDIDATE
In a bid to add color to the 2002 French presidential campaign, and to warn politicians against complacency, Serge Scotto tried to enter the name of his dog Saucisse as a rival candidate. But despite picking up over four percent of the vote in municipal elections in Marseille, Saucisse failed to obtain the necessary backing to oppose Jacques Chirac in the final stages of the presidential election.

EXPERT WITNESS
A police dog took the stand in a Pittsburgh, Pennsylvania, courtroom in 1994. The defense attorney tried to prove that the dog, not his client, was the aggressor in a fight.

PUNCH-DRUNK
A black bear in Baker Lake, Washington, was found passed out on a resort lawn. He got that way after stealing and drinking 36 cans of campers' beer!

GONE IN A FLASH
A single lightning strike on a farm in northern Israel killed an incredible 10,000 chickens.

HIGH MARKING
Giant pandas mark their territory by performing a handstand and urinating as high as possible up the side of a tree!

LOST AND FOUND
A dog that had been reported missing from his home in Columbus, Ohio, in 2002 turned up inside a 10-ft (3-m) long python that was found lurking under a neighbor's house. The neighbor called the police when she spotted the large snake with an ominous bulge in its middle.

HOLY CAT
Mike McGregor, from Edinburgh, Scotland, had never spotted anything unusual about the markings of his pet cat Brandy, until he saw Christ's face, just as it appears on the Turin Shroud, staring out at him. He said: "It's not every day that you see the face of Jesus in your cat's fur."

COW HIDE
It takes an incredible 3,000 cows to supply the National Football League with enough leather for just one season's worth of footballs!

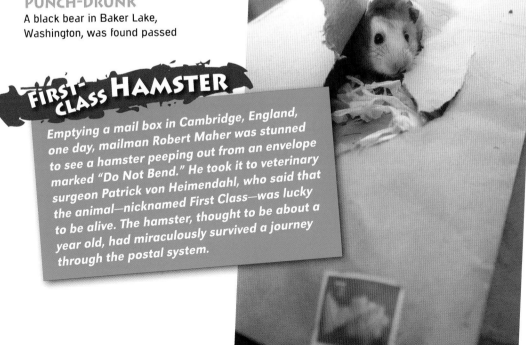

FIRST CLASS HAMSTER
Emptying a mail box in Cambridge, England, one day, mailman Robert Maher was stunned to see a hamster peeping out from an envelope marked "Do Not Bend." He took it to veterinary surgeon Patrick von Heimendahl, who said that the animal—nicknamed First Class—was lucky to be alive. The hamster, thought to be about a year old, had miraculously survived a journey through the postal system.

UNUSUAL PASSENGER

When a man rides a bike, it's nothing special, but when a dog rides a man who rides a bike, that is special! The dog is Spike, a Jack Russell terrier, who can be seen perched on the shoulders of his owner, Denton Walthall, as the latter cycles around the streets of Henrico, Virginia. Mr. Walthall explained how the unusual pose started: "One day I was calling him and he came running at a fast pace. I was squatting down to catch him but he flew up, landed on my leg and then scrambled up on my shoulder. And he was at home. Sometimes I try to get him down, but he simply positions himself further on my back so that he can stay there."

CATTLE WEDDING

In July 2005, a pair of dwarf Brahman cattle were married in a lavish Thai wedding ceremony. Krachang Kanokprasert, the owner of the bull, originally wanted to buy the bride, but when her owner refused to sell, the two farmers agreed to join the miniature breeding stock in matrimony.

MIGHTY PLUNGE

Sam, a German shepherd with California's Lodi Police Department, jumped 50 ft (15 m) into a river from a bridge while pursuing a suspect in 2001. Once in the water, Sam swam after the suspect and proceeded to herd him to his human colleagues.

ACTIVE ANTS

An ant colony built beneath Melbourne, Australia, in 2004 measured a staggering 60 mi (97 km) wide. The Argentine ants formed a giant supercolony as a result of co-operative behavior.

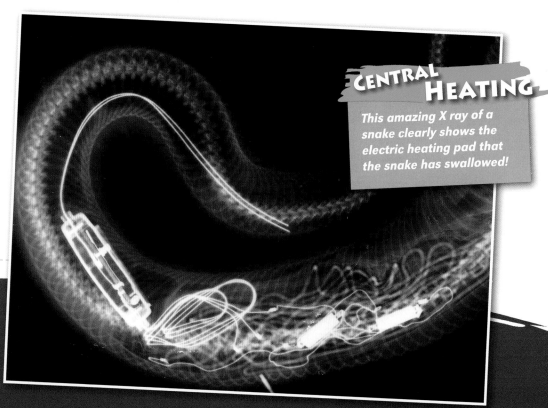

CENTRAL HEATING

This amazing X ray of a snake clearly shows the electric heating pad that the snake has swallowed!

HUMAN ZOO

In August 2005, visitors to England's London Zoo were in for a big surprise at the bear enclosure. Instead of black bears, prowling around on the rocky landscape were eight human beings wearing very little. The volunteers spent three days on Bear Mountain, entertaining themselves with games and music. The zoo explained that the exhibition was designed to show the basic nature of humans.

GREAT ESCAPE

Who let the dogs out? That's exactly what staff at Battersea Dogs' Home in London, England, wanted to know.

In 2004, several mornings in a row, staff arrived at Battersea Dogs' Home to find that as many as nine dogs had escaped from their compounds and were causing chaos in the kitchen. In a bid to solve the mystery of how the dogs managed to get free, the dogs' home installed video surveillance cameras. These revealed that a three-year-old Lurcher called Red had learned how not only to unbolt his own kennel door using his nose and teeth, but also how to to free his fellow hounds to join in the adventure, helping themselves to food in the kitchen.

Having studied how staff moved the bolt to unlock the kennel door, Red the lurcher used his teeth to do the same.

Please make sure my kennel door is always locked – I can open them!

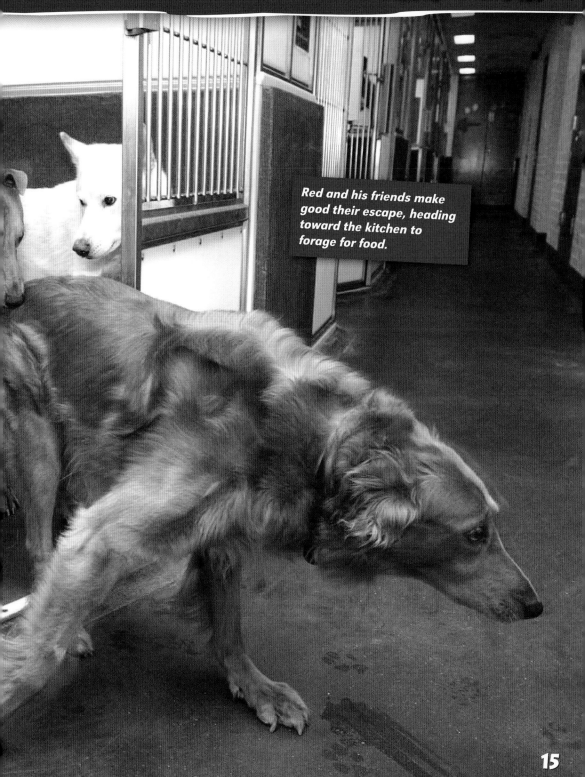

Red and his friends make good their escape, heading toward the kitchen to forage for food.

GREEN BEARS

In 2004, the usually white coats of Sheba and her son Inuka, Singapore Zoo's two polar bears, turned green! The color change was caused by harmless algae growing in the bears' hollow hair shafts, and was the result of Singapore's tropical climate. Both bears were successfully bleached with hydrogen peroxide.

WALKING OCTOPUS

Scientists in California have discovered an octopus that appears to walk on two legs! A species of the tiny tropical octopus has developed a technique whereby it wraps itself up into a ball and then releases just two of its eight tentacles so that it can "walk" backwards along the ocean floor.

CRAZY GATOR

An albino alligator at Blank Park Zoo in Des Moines, Iowa, turned pink when it became excited!

ROOSTER BOOSTER

Melvin the giant rooster just can't stop growing. At 18 months old, he stood 2 ft (60 cm) tall and weighed more than 15 lb (6.8 kg)—twice as much as other Buff Orpingtons.

His owner, Jeremy Goldsmith of Stansted, U.K., said: "We're staggered. No one's heard of a cockerel this big."

MIXED PARENTAGE

Nikita the foal earned her stripes soon after her birth in Morgenzon, South Africa, in 2004. Her mother, Linda, was a Shetland pony and her father, Jonny, was a zebra!

SWIMMING FOR DEER LIFE!

At a wildlife refuge in Georgia, Rangers saw a 13-ft (4-m) alligator that had attacked an adult deer and carried it off, swimming with the animal in its mouth!

PAW PRINTS

A talented tabby cat named Bud D. Holly, who lived with Sharon Flood at her art gallery in Mendocino, California, had a number of his paintings exhibited in 1992. Twenty of the works, created with paws and watercolors, were sold, some fetching over $100.

LARGE LITTER

Tia, a Neopolitan blue mastiff from the village of Manea in the U.K., gave birth to an amazing 24 puppies in January 2005. Four puppies died shortly after birth, but the remaining 20 were more than a handful—the puppies had to be bottle-fed every four hours! Fully grown the dogs will stand 2 ft (0.6 m) high.

FLYING DOG

Star of the 2002 Great American Mutt Show, held in Central Park, New York, was Rhoadi, a small brown dog who flew through the air on a bungee cord, reaching heights of more than 6 ft (2 m). Another contest at the show, which was open to only mongrels and strays, was for the dog that was the best kisser!

SNIFFER RAT

Gambian giant pouch rats are used to sniff out deadly landmines in Mozambique. The rats are trained to associate the smell of explosives with a food reward and indicate the potential danger to their handlers by frantically scratching the earth.

FLYING SNAKE

Believe it or not, there is a snake that flies! The little-known U.S. Navajo flying snake has lateral wing-like membranes running down its body, enabling it to glide through the air.

SCARY CREEPY CRAWLY

This enormous cockroach is an amazing 3 in (7.6 cm) long and weighs 1¼ oz (35 g). Found in Brisbane, Australia, in 1997, it now holds permanent residence at the Queensland Museum.

HAPPY SHOPPER

We've all heard of dogs that fetch newspapers or slippers. Well, J.C., a golden retriever from Penn Hills, Pennsylvania, goes a step further. He regularly fetches prescriptions for his owners, Chuck and Betty Pusateri, from a nearby drugstore.

TWO-NOSED DOG

There is a rare breed of dog in the Amazon basin that has two noses. The double-nosed Andean tiger hound was first described a century ago but, in 2005, an expedition led by British adventurer John Blashford-Snell came nose to noses with a specimen. Not surprisingly, the dogs are valued for their excellent sense of smell, which they use to hunt jaguars that prey on villagers' cattle.

BIG MOUTH

The North American opossum can open its mouth wider than 90 degrees when trying to scare away an attacker.

WELL-GROOMED

A Denton, Texas, firm called Groom Doggy offers tuxedos, bow ties, and wedding dresses for our canine friends. In fact the company has everything a dog could ever want to fulfill its formal-wear needs.

MY LITTLE PONY

Even miniature horses expect to reach a height of 3 ft (1 m) or more, but Peanut, the miniature dwarf stallion, stands just 20 in (51 cm) tall. He owes his diminutive stature to his mother, who was only 26 in (66 cm) tall.

BAMBOO CAST

Malai, a 98-year-old female elephant in Thailand, broke her leg in June 2005. Her trainers put a bamboo splint on her front leg in the hope that she would fully recover.

LEGAL ROOSTER

Charged with raising poultry without a permit, David Ashley appeared in court in Seneca Falls, New York, carrying a rooster. When the judge ordered the bird to be removed, Ashley replied that it was his attorney!

DUAL-SEX CRAB

In May 2005, a fisherman caught a blue crab in Chesapeake Bay, Virginia, that was female on one side and male on the other. Females have red-tipped claws, while males have blue—but this crab had one of each. Experts at the Virginia Institute of Marine Science said the crab was an extremely rare creature called a bilateral gynandromorph, meaning it is split between two genders. They said that the crab's condition probably resulted from a chromosomal mishap shortly after its conception.

DIVING PIG

Meet Miss Piggy, the amazing diving pig! Miss Piggy jumped into the record books in July 2005 when she dived 11 ft (3.3 m) into a pool from a platform 16 ft (5 m) high at Australia's Royal Darwin Show. Owner Tom Vandeleur, who had been training Miss Piggy for a month leading up to the show, said: "She does everything herself. She goes up the 16-ft (5-m) ramp herself, she dives herself."

REGULAR CUSTOMER

One of the best customers at The Chocolate Moose restaurant in Farmland, Indiana, is Missy Jo, a 60-lb (27-kg) bulldog. Even though she never actually sets foot inside the place, Missy Jo sits outside on the patio with owner Tony Mills for a daily treat of plain cheeseburgers and vanilla milkshakes!

UGLIEST DOG

In June 2005, a 14-year-old Chinese crested pedigree dog named Sam, won the title that no dog wants—World's Ugliest Dog. And this was the third year running that Sam had won the title. Until his death in November 2005, Sam was famous for his ugliness. He was pale-eyed and wrinkled, had a withered neck, and appeared to have almost no hair.

STILL LIFE

Californian taxidermist Tia Resleure, stuffs animals to create fairytale worlds where pigeons wear ball gowns, chickens tell fortunes—and even kittens are framed!

›IN‹ DEPTH

How did you get the idea to create art from dead animals?

"As a child I felt closer to our pets and farm animals than to my own family. I read *Alice in Wonderland* and wanted to morph into an animal. I inherited my grandfather's collection of taxidermy from Australia, where he grew up, and my father was always picking up bones—he once made a headdress out of a zebra head."

How did you learn how to create the animal art?

"I started using animal remains in my sculptures in the early eighties, but in 1998 I went on a two-week taxidermy course just to see if I had the nerve to work with fresh specimens."

What was the first piece you ever did, and do you have a favorite now?

"On that course, I did the "Mallard on a Circus Ball" and the "Fortune Telling Chicken." The director of the school

mocked me and said it was unnatural. I didn't think there was anything natural about a conventional duck flying against a piece of driftwood! My favorite piece is 'Little Shrill Voices,' which uses fetal kittens from a cat that had to undergo an emergency pregnancy spay."

What inspires your work?

"Old European curiosity cabinets, and French, German, and Russian fairy tales. When I'm working on my pieces, I imagine little stories for them."

Where do you get the animals you use?

"Because of my work in the animal welfare community, I have a lot of contacts with hobby and livestock breeders. Nothing is killed for my work— I just recycle animals that have already died."

Have you ever taxidermied your own pets?

"Yes. Part of the process of dealing with the loss of my pets is doing something with their remains. The first one I did was my first Italian greyhound, Aissi. I had to keep her in the freezer for about three years before I could start. The first time I pulled her out of the bag to let her thaw, my heart just clenched up. But then it all just went away and became very peaceful."

Do you have a future project you'd love to do?

"I have a huge old doll's house that I want to fill with animals. I want to fill the lowest level with moles, then ground-level animals on the next floor up, and little birds in the attic."

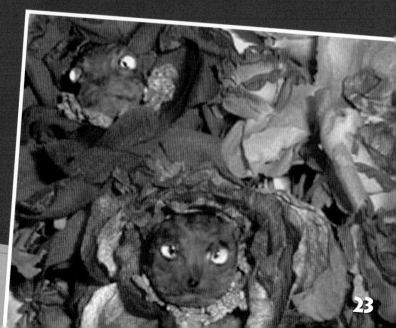

CAT CALL

After receiving an emergency call, police smashed down the door of a house in Auckland, New Zealand, in 2005—only to find that the call had been made by the homeowner's cat! The cat, named Tabby, had managed to contact the police while walking across the phone.

OPPORTUNITY KNOCKS

A bear in Croatia has learned how to trick householders into letting him into their homes by knocking at the door. Experts think that the 490-lb (222-kg) brown bear learned the ruse while nudging at a door in an attempt to get it open.

BURIED ALIVE

Thoughtful elephants in Kenya frequently bury sleeping hunters under leaves and piles of branches, thinking that the humans are dead.

TREE-CLIMBER

Ted, a four-year-old terrier, could climb 10 ft (3 m) up a tree and retrieve his ball. He was owned by Bill Vandever from Tulsa, Oklahoma.

MORE THAN A MOUTHFUL

Auggie was a dog who liked to do tricks with tennis balls. His owner Lauren Miller demonstrated his trick of picking up five tennis balls in his mouth at the same time!

DEADLY STRUGGLE

A 73-year-old Kenyan grandfather reached into the mouth of an attacking leopard and tore out its tongue to kill it. Farmer Daniel M'Mburugu was tending to his crops near Mount Kenya in June 2005 when the leopard leaped on him from long grass. As the leopard mauled him, M'Mburugu thrust his fist down the animal's throat and gradually managed to pull out its tongue, leaving the beast in its death throes. Hearing the screams, a neighbor soon arrived to finish the leopard off.

SNAPPED BACK

Cooper, a five-year-old golden retriever, managed to fight off a 14 ft (4.3 m), 700 lb (318 kg) alligator in a canal near Lake Moultrie, South Carolina, in June 2005. The dog was swimming across the canal when the reptile—three times Cooper's size—pounced. Cooper lost a few teeth and some skin, but the alligator retreated after being bitten repeatedly on the snout. Cooper's owner, Tom Kierspe, said afterward: "We've changed the dog's name to Lucky."

MONKEY BUSINESS

In Phoenix, Arizona, the SWAT team announced plans in 2005 to train a small monkey as a spy. The capuchin monkey will wear a bullet-proof vest, video camera, and two-way radio, and, intelligence experts hope, be able to access areas that no officer or robot could go.

MUDDY SWIM

For his act "Becoming Earthworm," performance artist Paul Hurley of the U.K. spent nine days in the mud and rain wearing only swimming trunks and goggles.

FISH SLAP

Marcy Poplett, of Peoria, Illinois, was injured and knocked off a personal watercraft on the Illinois River after a silver carp leaped out of the water and smacked her in the face!

UN-BEE-LIE-VABLE

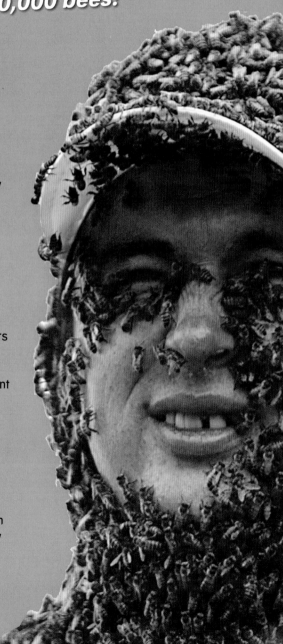

Marin Tellez created a buzz around the Colombian city of Bucaramanga in September 2005 when he covered his entire body in 500,000 bees!

Wearing just a cap and shorts, and no protective chemicals, the 35-year-old beekeeper allowed the aggressive Africanized bees to swarm all over him for two whole hours.

Once the queen bee had landed on Tellez, the rest of the colony followed on behind her, guided by her scent. Spectators were kept 30 ft (9 m) from the platform to avoid being stung, while other beekeepers stood by wearing protective suits and carrying smoke canisters in case of emergency.

Tellez explained: "I have been working with beehives for 23 years and I know how bees behave. I have to be very calm to transmit that serenity to them and to prevent them from hurting me."

He claims to have been stung so many times that his body has built up some resistance to the potentially lethal formic acid. His worst experience was being attacked by more than 150 bees when he was just 17 years old. On that occasion he saved himself by jumping into a water tank.

Tellez claims that the key to his success was, perhaps unsurprisingly, staying very calm! The bees, he says, picked up on this, and just went about their ordinary business.

Once the queen bee had landed on Tellez, the other 499,999 followed, coating the beekeeper's entire body with their swarm.

SKATEBOARDING DOG

Few sporting pets are more accomplished than Tyson the skateboarding bulldog. Tyson, from Huntington Beach, California, skates every day and is able to get on the board unaided. He runs with two paws on the tarmac and uses the other two to steer his skateboard. Then, as soon as he reaches a decent speed, he jumps aboard properly and skates for his life.

MILLI-MAGIC

Capuchin monkeys use an unusual natural mosquito repellent—they rub themselves with millipedes.

FREAK FETUS

A two-headed moose fetus, which measured about 1 ft (30 cm) long, was discovered in Alaska in 2002 after the animal's mother had been shot by a hunter.

GREAT SURVIVOR

Talbot, a six-month-old stray cat, wandered into a car plant at Ryton, England, in 1999, and went to sleep in the body shell of a Peugeot 206 on the assembly line. With the cat still asleep inside, the shell then went into the paint-baking oven at a temperature of 145°F (63°C)! Amazingly, he survived, although his paw pads were completely burned off and his fur was singed.

LITTER-KWITTER

No more unpleasant messy litter trays with the Litter-Kwitter, the ingenious invention that trains household cats to use the same toilet as their owners. Three disks slide into a seat-like device that can be positioned on the toilet bowl. The red, amber, and green disks have progressively larger bowls with smaller amounts of cat litter in them to help the cats adjust to using their owner's toilet.

FRIENDS REUNITED

Seven years after going missing from her Florida home, Cheyenne the cat was reunited with owner Pamela Edwards in 2004—after being found 2,800 mi (4,500 km) away in San Francisco.

PIG OLYMPICS

In April 2005, thousands of Shanghai residents trotted out to a city park to watch a herd of miniature pigs compete in what organizers called the "Pig Olympics."

Piglets race down a track, jostling and jumping for key positions in the hurdle race.

The pigs, a midget species from Thailand, begin training soon after birth and can start performing when they are a year old. They learn to run over hurdles, jump through hoops, dive into water, and swim—in fact, these amazing sporting pigs can do almost anything... except fly.

Two piglets compete in the swimming race.

31

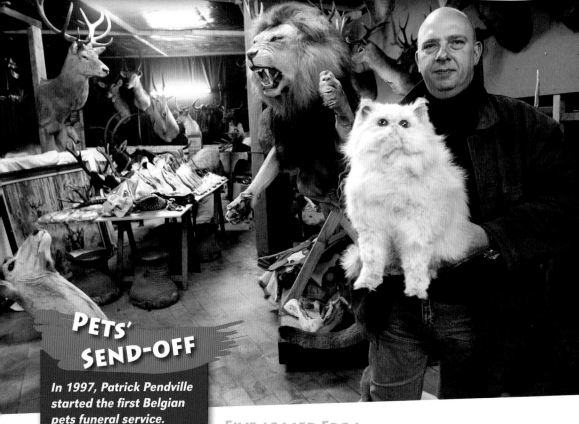

PETS' SEND-OFF

In 1997, Patrick Pendville started the first Belgian pets funeral service. Animatrans, as it is known, offers transport, burial, individual or collective certified cremation, collection of ashes, taxidermy, facial masks, and urns. About 1,200 animals pass through the doors every year. His customers bring not only cats and dogs, but other animals such as birds, goats, horses, and sheep—and even exotic breeds, such as crocodiles, tigers, snakes, and monkeys.

FIVE-LEGGED FROG

In August 2004, nine-year-old Cori Praska found a five-legged frog with 23 toes near Stewartville, Minnesota. Three of the frog's legs appeared normal, but the fourth had another leg as an offshoot, with its own three feet attached to it.

BACK TO WORK

At the start of the 20th century, when sheep still grazed in New York's Central Park, a collie named Shep had the job of controlling the flock. When Shep was retired he was sent to a farm 40 mi (64 km) away in upstate New York. However, the determined dog quickly escaped and, even though he had never previously been beyond Manhattan, managed to find his way back to the Big Apple by first stowing away on a ferry that would take him to Manhattan Island, and then sniffing his way back from 42nd Street to Central Park!

HEALING PAWS

In the 1980s, Jane Bailey, of Lyme Regis, England, owned a cat named Rogan that was said to have healing powers. By "laying paws" on his patients' bodies, the cat was apparently able to cure sufferers of arthritis and back injuries. He became so famous that up to 90 people a week sought his help. His fur, which was combed daily, also possessed special properties and Jane would send parcels of it to those in need.

LONG TREK

In 1923, Bobbie the collie became separated from his family on a visit to Indiana. Lost and alone, he returned to the family home in Silverton, Oregon, six months later, having walked a staggering 2,800 mi (4,500 km) across seven states!

GORILLA TALK

Born in 1971, Koko the gorilla has appeared in *The New York Times* and on the cover of several prestigious magazines. Three books have been written about her, and scientists hang on her every word. She has even had her life story told on TV. For Koko, who lives at the Gorilla Foundation in Woodside, California, can communicate with humans. The 35-year-old primate has been taught sign language since she was an infant by Dr. Francine (Penny) Patterson and has now mastered more than 1,000 words. In addition, she understands around 2,000 words of spoken English and has a tested IQ of between 70 and 90 on a human scale where 100 is considered normal. Koko has also learned to use a camera and loves the telephone.

PARROT BANNED

In November 1994, a defense lawyer in San Francisco, California, wanted to call a parrot to the witness stand in the hope that the bird would speak the name of the man who killed its owner. However, the judge refused to allow it.

HAIRY HORSE

An extraordinary horse from California had a 14-ft (4.3-m) mane and 13-ft (4-m) tail.

HELPING HOOVES

Shoppers in Raleigh, North Carolina, have been witnessing some unusual sights around town—namely miniature horses, 24 in (61 cm) tall, wearing sneakers and warm blankets. These horses are the equine version of guide dogs and are being put through their paces in busy shopping malls. Janet and Don Burleson began training mini horses to help blind and visually impaired people in 1999.

MINI CAT
A blue point Himalayan cat from the U.S.A. called Tinker Toy was just 2¾ in (7 cm) tall at the shoulder and 7½ in (19 cm) long–about the size of a check book.

BABY-DRY DIAPER
Dr. Kobi Assaf, of Jerusalem's Hadassah Hospital, once treated a 12-month-old baby boy who survived a venomous snake bite because the boy's diaper absorbed the venom.

TRUMPET TUNES
Thailand's elephant orchestra has 12 jumbo elephants playing oversized instruments! Their last CD sold 7,000 copies in the U.S.A. alone.

COMPUTER BLIP
In 1988, Mastercard sent a letter to Fustuce Ringgenburg, of Hemet, California, with the offer of a $5,000 credit limit, unaware that Fustuce was in fact the family cat.

GREAT TREK
In 1953, Sugar, a Persian cat, trekked 1,500 mi (2,414 km) from Anderson, California, to Gage, Oklahoma, after her owners had moved there. The family had left the cat with a friend because of her bad hip, but despite the injury Sugar made a 14-month journey to be reunited with them.

CAT ON A HOT TIN ROOF

Torri Hutchinson was driving along the highway near Inkom, Idaho, in 2005 when a fellow motorist alerted her to the fact that her cat was on the car roof. Hutchinson, Torri's orange tabby, had been clinging to the roof for 10 mi (16 km). Torri hadn't even noticed the cat when she stopped for gas!

KISS OF LIFE

When one of Eugene Safken's young chickens appeared to have drowned in a tub in 2005, the Colorado farmer saved the bird by giving it mouth-to-beak resuscitation! After swinging the chicken by the feet in an attempt to revive it, he blew into its beak until the bird began to chirp. The farmer said: "I started yelling, 'You're too young to die!' And every time I'd yell, he'd chirp."

DÉJÀ VU

A Canadian sailor and his dog were rescued from the same island twice in a week in May 2002. Melvin Cote was hoping to spend the summer in the Queen Charlotte Islands, British Columbia, but severe weather capsized his boat. After the rescue, Cote and his dog sailed back to the shipwreck to salvage their things, but sank again in the same spot!

KENNEL OF LOVE

The doggy love motel, complete with a heart-shaped mirror on the ceiling and a headboard resembling a dog bone, opened in August 2005 for loving doggy couples. Billy and Jully, two Yorkshire terriers, stayed at the pet motel in Sao Paulo, Brazil. The air-conditioned room has a paw-print decorative motif, special control panels to dim the lights, romantic music, and films that can be screened. The rooms cost 100 reais ($54) for two hours.

LANGUAGE PROBLEM

A customer at a pet shop in Napierville, Quebec, threatened to report the shop to the Canadian government's French-language monitoring office in 1996 after being shown a parrot that spoke only English.

SHARK ESCAPE

Dolphins rescued four swimmers off the New Zealand coast by encircling them for 40 minutes while a great white shark swam nearby!

EQUINE ALLERGY

Teddy the horse has to sleep on shredded newspaper, because he has an allergy to, of all things, hay! If the horse is exposed to hay or straw, he immediately starts coughing and sneezing in an equine version of hay fever. His owner, Samantha Ashby, from Coventry, England, also has to damp down his feed to remove any dust spores.

TRENDY TERRIER

New York boutique-owner Heather Nicosia ensures that her Yorkshire terrier Woody is one of the most fashionable dogs in town. She makes him his own line of WoodyWear clothes and dresses him in a range of trendy outfits ranging from pajamas to Batman and Spiderman costumes.

FANTASTIC FISH

Bruce, an Oranda goldfish, measures a staggering 17.1 in (43.5 cm) from snout to tail fin! Named after the late kung fu star Bruce Lee, Bruce swims with normal-sized goldfish at Shanghai Ocean Aquarium.

FISHY KISS

In 1998, Dan Heath, of Medford, Oregon, could barely believe his eyes when he saw Chino, his golden retriever, standing over a fishpond, nose to nose with Falstaff, an orange-and-black carp. Each day, Chino sprints out to the backyard, peers into the water and waits. Within seconds, Falstaff pops up and the two gently touch noses. Heath doesn't know how or why Chino and Falstaff became friends, but it's obvious to everyone that their friendship is watertight.

YOUNG AND OLD

A baby hippo, weighing about 660 lb (300 kg), was orphaned when the Asian tsunami in December 2004 washed away his mother. Named Owen, he has been adopted by a 120-year-old tortoise, Mzee. Owen was spotted on the coast and taken to the Haller Park in Mombasa, Kenya. There are other hippos at the Park, but on his arrival he made straight for the ancient tortoise and the pair are now inseparable! Owen often lays his head on Mzee's shell to rest when he's tired.

BEAR'S BREATH

In May 2005, vets at Seneca Park Zoo, Rochester, New York, used a hammer and chisel to remove an infected tooth from the mouth of an 805-lb (365-kg) polar bear named Yukon. The tooth had been giving the bear bad breath.

RESOURCEFUL HAMSTER

Two house moves and some years after thinking they had lost their pet hamster, the Cummins family, from Edmonton, Alberta, were amazed when it reappeared. It turned out that the hamster had never actually left home

but had burrowed into the sofa, using it as a nest. The animal had survived by sneaking out at night and taking food and water from the bowls of the family's other pets.

JUMBO ARTIST

The biggest draw at Taman Safari Park in Bogor, Indonesia, is Windi the artistic elephant. By holding on to the brush with her trunk, she dabs the paint on the canvas to form her own forest of colors. In her first six months at the park, the 18-year-old female created 50 paintings, many of which sold at over 20,000 Indonesian rupiahs ($2) each. Others were exhibited outside the park's restaurant.

INVISIBLE BEARS

Polar bears are so well insulated they are almost invisible to infrared cameras.

FIVE-LEGGED DOG

Believe it or not, a five-legged dog was found near a state park near Raleigh, North Carolina, in November 2003. Although it was previously unheard of for such an animal to live much past birth, this dog—a Maltese-terrier mix named Popcorn—was at least nine months old. A vet removed the extra leg because it was hampering the dog's movement, as well as another rear leg that rotated at a 90-degree angle, making it useless. The dog with five legs became a dog with only three.

INDIAN MARKING

This horse, owned by J.F. Daniel and R.L. Anderson, of Craigsville, Virginia, had a marking on its neck in the shape of an American Indian head.

FROG-LIFTER

Bill Steed, professor of Frog Psychology at Croaker College, Emeryville, California, trained frogs to lift barbells.

MOTHER'S MILK

A dog feeds two tiger cubs at a zoo in Hefei, China, in May 2005. The tigers' mother did not have enough milk to feed the cubs, so the zookeepers found a dog to act as wet nurse.

EAGER BEAVERS

Police searching for stolen money in Greensburg, Los Angeles, discovered beavers had found the money in their creek and woven thousands of dollars into their dam!

FERRET LOVER

C.J. Jones is mad about ferrets. After falling in love with an injured ferret that was brought to the animal hospital where she worked, C.J. opened her home to the furry little creatures, and in 1997 founded the "24 Carat Ferret Rescue and Shelter" in Las Vegas, Nevada. She looks after a maximun of 90 ferrets at a time and has rescued more than 1,500 so far in total.

MAYOR HEE-HAW

The small town of Florissant, Colombia, elected Paco Bell as its mayor. Believe it or not, he is a donkey!

JUMPING JACK

Jack, a six-year-old terrier, gained notoriety when he was banned from darts tournaments in a Welsh pub in 2001, because after each round he kept jumping up to the board, snatching the darts, and then running off with them. In his youth Jack could reach the height of the bull's eye (5 ft 8 in/1.73 m) with ease and would even snatch darts that had landed at the very top of the board.

SPEAKING CAT

Pala, a black-and-white tomcat that lived in the Turkish town of Konya in the 1960s, had a vocabulary equivalent to that of a one-year-old baby. His owner, Eyup Mutluturk, explained that the cat began talking after becoming jealous of the attention lavished upon the family's grandchildren and was able to speak freely in Turkish.

DOGGY BEACH

Bau Beach, north of the Italian capital, Rome, is a beach with a difference. Opened in 2000, it has been designed specially for dogs. Most Italian beaches ban dogs, but here for 5 euros ($6) they are given an umbrella, a towel, and a dog bowl, and their owners are handed a shovel to clean up any mess. After frolicking happily in the waves, the dogs can also take a shower under a high-pressured hose.

BULL CHASE

Despite six instances of human pile-ups, often injuring more than a hundred people, during the annual Running of the Bulls in Pamplona, Spain, since 1900, only 15 people have lost their lives.

BARK PARK!

Dog Bark Park is home to Toby and Sweet Willy. Toby is a 12-ft (3.7-m) statue and Sweet Willy, officially known as Dog Bark Park Inn, is a bed-and-breakfast establishment where guests can enter the body of the beagle to sleep. Alternatively, they can enjoy curling up in the cosy reading place in the dog's muzzle.

LIZARD LOUNGERS

Henry Lizardlover shares his Hollywood home with 35 lizards and takes amazing pictures of them in human poses. He loves them so much he even changed his name for them!

IN DEPTH

How long have you shared your house with lizards?

"Since 1981. I have a large house with separate rooms for the lizards—they don't live in cages so they get used to people. That's my secret."

Why the change of name?

"I changed my surname from Schiff to Lizardlover in the early eighties. I wanted to show my love and dedication to the lizards. I resented the stereotype that they are creepy-crawly and evil, and felt that by taking that name I was making myself a part of the lizard family."

How do you get the lizards to pose for pictures?

"If a lizard is calm and trusts you, it will demonstrate remarkably intelligent behavior, and will be happy to maintain these posed positions for up to an hour on furniture that he or she finds comfortable."

Do you have to train them?

"Not at all. I give them a comfortable room to hang out in, they see me come and go every day in a graceful and non-threatening way. They recognize that I am a friendly creature."

What are your favorite lizard pictures?

"A favorite is of Hasbro, an iguana I used to have, holding a guitar and singing into a microphone. There's also one of a big iguana cradling another in his arms—to portray that they can be loving to each other. My top models for postcards and calendars include iguanas Lovable and Prince Charming, and Chinese Water Dragons Larry Love, Laura Love, and Lana Love."

They pose like humans—do they behave that way too?

"I used to take some out to a parking lot to sunbathe—after 20 minutes they would walk back to my truck and get back in on their own. Hasbro used to scratch at night on my bedroom door, get into my bed, and go to sleep. In the morning this lizard, weighing 20 lb, and measuring 6 ft in length, would lie on my chest or, if it was chilly, poke his nose underneath the blanket."

Does everyone love what you do?

"Some people can't believe the lizards are real, or they say I drug them, hypnotize them, put them in the refrigerator first, or paralyze them. They say they can't breathe when they're posing—it's all untrue. They're calm and relaxed—scared lizards run around and bounce off the walls."

Could anyone do what you do with lizards?

"Not all act the way mine do. Male adult iguanas can be dangerous if they are in breeding season moods, they can confuse humans for other male iguanas and become violent. They can attack, rip flesh, or bite off a section of nose. You have to read their body language carefully."

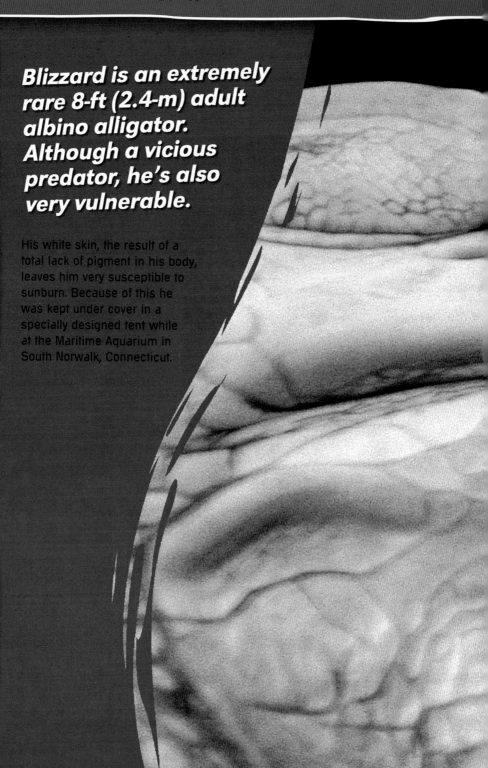

PALE SCALES

Blizzard is an extremely rare 8-ft (2.4-m) adult albino alligator. Although a vicious predator, he's also very vulnerable.

His white skin, the result of a total lack of pigment in his body, leaves him very susceptible to sunburn. Because of this he was kept under cover in a specially designed tent while at the Maritime Aquarium in South Norwalk, Connecticut.

MINI MARVEL

Each fall, despite weighing just 0.2 oz (6 g), the ruby-throated hummingbird propels its tiny body, only 3½ in (9 cm) long, on a nonstop 500-mi (805-km) flight from North America across the Gulf of Mexico to South America.

LAP OF LUXURY

Under the terms of their owner's will, Chihuahua Frankie and cats Ani and Pepe Le Pew live in a $20 million San Diego mansion while their caregiver lives in a small apartment.

FLIGHT OF FANCY

Pigeon-lover John Elsworth, of Houston, Texas, decided to propose to his girlfriend via a message delivered by homing pigeon. But the bird got lost and took the note instead to the home of Rita Williams. Rita invited John over and they fell in love and got married.

A LOT OF LOBSTER

At the Weathervane Restaurant lobster-eating competition in 2004, Barry Giddings, of Chester, Vermont, devoured 19 lobsters in 35 minutes!

CHICKEN WALK

Twenty chickens strutted their stuff on a Japanese catwalk in the latest styles for the fashion-conscious hen. A range of clothing, by Austrian designer Edgar Honetschlaeger, caters for sizes small, medium, large, extra large, and turkey.

KANGAROO BAR

Boomer, an 18-month-old orphaned kangaroo, is fed peanuts by Kathy Noble, owner of the Comet Inn in Hartley Vale, Australia. In 2005, the baby kangaroo was found inside the pouch of his dead mother on the side of the road. After rearing, Boomer decided he liked the bar so much that he is now a regular visitor.

MONKEY BUSINESS

U.S. showbiz chimp Mr. Jiggs (who was actually female) was not everybody's favorite ape. On her way to entertain at a Scout jamboree, and accompanied by her trainer Ronald Winters, Mr. Jiggs walked into a bar at Freehold, New Jersey, wearing full Boy Scout's uniform. The shock caused customer Joan Hemmer to drop her drink, fall against a wall, and injure her shoulder. She sued Winters, but lost.

FRISBEE CHAMPION

Dog Ashley Whippet was such an accomplished Frisbee catcher that he was invited to appear at the 1974 World Frisbee Championships, which had previously been for humans only. Captivated by his display, the WFC devised a Catch and Fetch competition for dogs, of which Ashley became the first world champion. He performed at the Super Bowl and at the White House, and upon his death in 1985 he received a tribute in Sports Illustrated.

DOG GIOVANNI

Australian opera singer Judith Dodsworth is never short of an accompaniment—even if it is provided by her pet greyhound, Pikelet. Ms. Dodsworth says the canine virtuoso began copying her during rehearsals and hasn't stopped singing since. "As soon as I opened my mouth, he started singing. He's not bad but he's pretty loud and pretty high." And Pikelet's favorite composer? Pooch-ini, of course!

STRANGE BEDFELLOWS

Rattlesnakes hibernate through winter in groups of up to 1,000. Amazingly, they often share a site with prairie dogs—their favorite prey when they are not in hibernation.

ACKNOWLEDGMENTS

FRONT COVER (t/l) Erik S.Lesser, (c/l) © John Anderson – iStock.com, (sp) Stewart Cook/Rex Features; 4 (l) © John Anderson – iStock.com, (r) Stewart Cook/Rex Features; 5 (r) Erik S.Lesser; 8–9 Anna Kelly; 9 (t) © John Anderson – iStock.com; 10 Reuters/Romeo Ranoco; 11 Rex Features; 13 Reuters/Stephen Hird; 14–15 Rex Features; 16–17 M. Usher/Rex Features; 18 Reuters/Str Old; 19 Sam Barcroft/Barcroft Media; 20 Reuters/Sukree Sukplang; 21 KPA/Zuma/Rex Features; 22–23 www.aCaseofCuriosities.com; 26–27 Reuters/Eliana Aponte; 28 Stewart Cook/Rex Features; 29 Rex Features; 30–31 Reuters/Claro Cortes; 32 Reuters/Thierry Roge; 34 Erik S.Lesser; 35 Reuters/STR New; 36–37 Reuters/Claro Cortes; 38 Gary Roberts/Rex Features 40 Reuters/China Daily Information Corp-CDIC; 41 Reuters/STR New; 42–43 Westley Hargraves/Barcroft Media; 44–45 Mary Schwalm/AP/PA Photos; 46 Masatoshi Okauchi/Rex Features; 47 Reuters/David Gray

KEY t = top, b = bottom, c = center, l = left, r = right, sp = single page, dp = double page

All other photos are from Ripley's Entertainment Inc.
Every attempt has been made to acknowledge correctly and contact copyright holders and we apologize in advance for any unintentional errors or omissions, which will be corrected in future editions.